The Paleo Kids
Cookbook

The Paleo Kids Cookbook

Transition Your Family to Delicious Grain- and Gluten-Free Food for a Lifetime of Healthy Eating

Jennifer Robins

bestselling author of *Down South Paleo* and *The New Yiddish Kitchen*

PAGE STREET
PUBLISHING CO.

PAGE STREET
PUBLISHING CO.

First published in 2016 by
Page Street Publishing Co.
27 Congress Street, Suite 103
Salem, MA 01970
www.pagestreetpublishing.com

Distributed by Macmillan, sales in Canada by The Canadian Manda Group.

19 18 17 16   1 2 3 4 5

ISBN-13: 978-1-62414-287-1
ISBN-10: 1-62414-287-7

Library of Congress Control Number: 2015960299

Cover and book design by Page Street Publishing Co.
Photography by Jennifer Robins and Jeremy Meek

Printed and bound in China

Page Street is proud to be a member of 1% for the Planet. Members donate one percent
of their sales to one or more of the over 1,500 environmental and sustainability charities
across the globe who participate in this program.

To all of the children whose dietary restrictions created division, isolation or sacrifice. May these recipes bring you comfort, inclusion and joy in both your healthful journeys and life's many celebrations.

Contents

Foreword by Dr. Tracy Freeman   9
Introduction   10
Tips for Transitioning   12

GOOD MORNING, SUNSHINE   17

Allergy-Friendly Waffles   18
Egg in a Hole   21
Grain- + Nut-Free Granola   22
Fruit Kabobs with Dairy-Free Dip   25
French Toast Sticks   26
Sausage Quiche   29
Cocoa 'N' Oatmeal   30
Cinnamon Maple Plantains   33
Silver Dollar Chocolate Chip Pancakes   34
Pale-O's Cereal   37
Green Eggs + Ham Roll Ups   38

MAIN SQUEEZE   41

Glazed Grain-Free Meatloaf + Crispy Onion Topping   42
Veggie Spaghetti and Meatballs   45
Crispy Sweet Potato Fish Sticks   46
Chicken Nuggets   49
Mini Pizzas   50
Grilled "Cheese"   53
Chicken Zoodle Soup   54
Liver Lovin' Turkey Burger Sliders   57
Meat Pockets   58
Ham + "Cheese" Quesadillas   61
Pizza Pockets   62
Mac 'N' "Cheese"   65
Grain-Free Corn Dog Dippers   66
Teriyaki Meatballs + Daikon Noodles   69

HEALING FOODS   71

Bone Broth   72
Banana Pudding   75
Cinnamon Applesauce   76
Ginger Chews   79
Dairy-Free Coconut Yogurt   80
Creamy Papaya"sick"les with Electrolytes   83
Flu Season Gummies   84

SNACK ATTACK   87

Ladybug Veggie Bites   88
Great Grape Gummies   91
Lala Truffles   92
Vanilla Wafers   95
Orange Dreamysicle Gummies   96
Graham Crackers   99
"Cheese" Quackers   100
Gummy Worms   103
Animal Crackers   104
Soft Pretzels   107
Monkey Toes (Filled Dates)   108
Critters on a Log + Homemade Sunflower Seed Butter 111
Paleo Piggies   112
Apple Cars + Caramel Dip   115

SIDEKICKS   117

Sweet Potato Bacon Tots   118
Parsnip Fries   121
Mimi's Little Veggie Trees   122
Give Peas a Chance Fritters   125
Veggie Rice + Gravy   126
BFF Brussels   129
Zucchini Sticks   130

SUPERHERO SMOOTHIES 133

Orange Berry Banshee	134
Crantastic Trio	137
Green Goblin	138
Strawberry Superpower	141
The Great Caped Grape	142
Pineapple Phantom	145

BREADS 'N' SUCH 147

Legit Sandwich Bread	148
Everyday Crackers	151
Mini Muffins	152
Weeknight Paleo Tortillas	155
Sweet Potato Slider Buns	156
Tortilla Chips	159
Pizza Crust	160
Homemade Grain-Free Pasta	163
Crispy Taco Shells	164
Hot Dog Buns	167

SIPS 'N' DIPS 169

Honey Mustard	170
Ranch Dressing	173
Ketchup	174
Awesome Sauce	177
Easy Pizza Sauce	178
Flax Milk	181
Sunflower Seed Milk	181
Chocolate Non Dairy Milk with Variations	181
Perfectly Pink Lemonade	182
Cheesy Dip	185
Salsa	186
Mayonnaise	189
BBQ Sauce	190
Rockin' Guacamole	193
Dairy-Free Butter	194
Coconut Whipped Cream	197
Hot Chocolate	198

TREATS 201

Brownies	202
Pudding Dirt in a Cup	205
S'mores	206
"Peanot" Butter Chocolate Chip Cookies	209
Double Chocolate Layer Cake	210
Brown Sugar Cinnamon Toasted Pastry	213
Anything-But-Basic Vanilla Cupcakes + Bettercream Frosting	214
Cake Pops	217
Mint Chocolate Chip Ice Cream	218
Strawberry Shortcake Bites	221
Funnel Cakes	222

LUNCH BUNCH 224

CAVEBABY'S FIRST FOODS 231

Acknowledgments	233
About the Author	235
Index	236

Foreword by Dr. Tracy Freeman

As parents, many of us are noticing that our children are struggling with their health. There are rampant allergies, focus and attention issues, and obesity to contend with. Parents today must seek solutions to their children's health that were not a consideration a generation prior. The connection between the environment and well-being is debatable, and many embattled parents are too weary to decipher why they are in this situation. The many variables including medications and therapies must be addressed. The one experiment that parents can control is the child's diet. Quality foods can be introduced that impact the brain, gastrointestinal tract and body as a whole. The hurdle we face as parents is making a tasty but healthy meal. Thank goodness Jennifer Robins lights the way with creative and kid-friendly meals!

I first met Jennifer as her physician. I have been impressed with her ability to educate herself on her journey to wellness. She has used her diet as a tool to rein in her autoimmune and endocrine issues, as well as infections like Lyme and chronic viruses. All of this while raising three small children, an awesome feat indeed. She has studied the impact of food on the immune system and created a genre of food that satisfies those with hypoallergenic needs. While it has truly been an honor to witness this healing quest, the best part has been tasting her food. After years of eating tasteless and boring food, the true miracle is that my kids love it too!

I have personally been on this trial-and-error journey with my own family. My children's food sensitivities and allergies eliminate many of the foods I grew up eating. When my autistic son was a toddler and I first embarked on this path, I would spend hours in Whole Foods studying labels looking for tolerated ingredients that are not camouflaged in sugar. In a stepwise fashion, I learned to create my own meals—one new ingredient at a time. With several horrible tasting creations behind me, I was excited to use Jen's recipes. The best part is that my kids don't feel as if they are missing out. In a world with ferocious food advertisements, children know when they are eating something different. I have worked hard to teach my children to know what foods are "junk." They get it, but they still sometimes want what other kids are eating. Jennifer's recipes have brought balance to my home. They can eat it, and more importantly, enjoy it.

As a physician, I see many conditions in which diet changes are essential. Food in our culture is seen as more than fuel for our bodies. It is how we socialize and a tool to form happy memories. We have associations with the flavors we taste and how we feel emotionally. Asking patients to eliminate foods they have become accustomed to is difficult. I stress the importance of small steps in this pursuit and the realization that each individual is different in their nutritional and medicinal needs. While not all of my patients chose a Paleolithic diet approach, many do. Others will use many aspects of the "Paleo" lifestyle. I have seen gastrointestinal and metabolic improvements from this practice. Most are especially excited with the weight loss. I have referred many of these patients to Jen's blog, www.predominantlyPaleo.com, where they can find food that satiates them physically and satisfies the need to find pleasure in their meals.

While the beneficial effects of clean dieting have been known for decades, the advent of new research has shown that returning the intestinal system to health is the cornerstone of a new paradigm in wellness. Allowing the body to heal itself by giving it the food and supportive environment in which to do so is the new mantra of the modern and open-minded physician. I am encouraged by the improvements in my patients, and I am continually amazed at the young palates that have adjusted to and thrived on a "predominantly Paleo" diet. Using Jennifer's approach and recipes found in this book, parents will be guided toward their goal of feeding their children unprocessed foods that enable kids to enjoy their meals while also nourishing their bodies.

Introduction

So you're finally ready for change! Or maybe you've been ready but just can't figure out where to start. Or maybe you've started but have been so overwhelmed by trying to feed your family "health" foods that you jumped ship before your kids could say "ewwww, that's gross!" Or even still, maybe you DO feel like you're doing a pretty darn fine job of feeding your family whole foods, but you're struggling to find recipes that are family-friendly, health-oriented AND accomplish the delicious factor we all want to achieve.

Here's the part where I'm extra honest with you...I fed my kids chicken nuggets, fish-shaped crackers, cow's milk by the gallon and vanilla wafers. I visited fast food joints on occasion, and I made pasta as if my family owned stock in Italy. I also fed them organic baby food and not-so-organic food. I breast fed, I bottle fed and basically just tried to do whatever I could to keep them alive and well. As a military family we have often been in survival mode, and I was content just to know they were under my watch and otherwise safe from harm.

My children have been healthy overall, at least from the outside. They were energetic toddlers who didn't suffer from much more than a snotty nose, and they missed very few days of school. But I noticed something else in them. While I was experiencing my own health crisis, I began to take note of chronic issues in my kids. My son (first born) had intense stomachaches, so much so he would cry out in pain, writhing around. My eldest daughter was diagnosed with sleep apnea at age five and had tonsils so enlarged they almost "kissed." And my youngest daughter had swollen lymph nodes in both her groin and her neck, so obvious you could see them without even palpating. I'd ask various pediatricians as we moved around the country, and the feedback was all too familiar. "Some kids just have this." "Oh, that's normal!" "Nothing to worry about there!"

This wasn't good enough for me. After all of my autoimmune diagnoses, chronic infections like Lyme disease and over 20 different labels in my medical files, I knew it was time to take action with my children. While they were by no means "sickly," I felt my own terrible health experiences were enough to initiate change with them as well.

It all began with gluten. After discovering I was gluten intolerant during my Hashimoto's diagnosis, I had both of my older kids tested (by stool) and was not surprised to find that they also created the antibodies against gluten in their digestive tracts. I took each child off of gluten by the age of two. I repeated this process with my youngest child, who also tested positive for gluten intolerance and eventually casein intolerance. Needless to say, after unveiling my own gluten and dairy sensitivities and seeing the evolution of my children's symptoms, I took them off dairy as well, especially after surgery was ultimately recommended for my snoring beauty.

In only weeks, I watched every last symptom clear from them. No more enlarged lymph nodes, no more snoring, no more mucus or tummy aches. In fact, I could not detect any residual issues whatsoever. Granted, as mentioned earlier, they were not sickly to begin with in terms of missing school or feeling terrible. Their symptoms were sort of "under the radar" warning signs to me, which I believe could have become much worse in time, similar to how my own issues crept up on me.

Then and there, I became a believer if ever there was any doubt (which there never really was). I watched change sweep across my family. And while other kids we knew had ear tubes, tonsillectomies, daily laxatives or monthly antibiotics, we took a turn that breathed new life into these little bodies I birthed.

It is important to note that I am not making medical claims, I do not believe that food fixes all and I understand that there is a role for all facets of healthcare. I am not recommending that you impersonate a healthcare practitioner, throw caution to the wind and start creating your own potions and elixirs. I do believe, however, that food has the incredible power to strengthen our immune systems, to nourish us and to heal us in a variety of ways. Alternatively, the wrong foods hold the power to destroy our digestive tracts (where much of our immune system resides), create inflammation and pain in our bodies and allow the overgrowth of microbes, which need to be kept in balance.

So why did I write *The Paleo Kids Cookbook* anyway?! Well, I'm so glad you asked. I wanted to help you finally get the good stuff into your littles, help you minimize arguments over food and bring back joy to mealtime. And here's the thing, if your kid is already eating kale and liver, then I celebrate you and your child's diverse palate! I think that's incredibly exciting. It's also not the story of all children. Kids have texture preferences, color preferences and are creatures of habit. They can be resistant to change and are certainly not shy to tell you about that <insert hysterics here.>

I wrote this book as a resource to help you transition your child off of mainstream favorites like tan foods and processed goop. I want to help you introduce new foods to your kiddo's diet and also sneak in some added nutrient-dense foods when the willingness to try new foods is not quite there yet. I have three children of my own who have eaten everywhere along the spectrum from healthy to horrid and can certainly be picky themselves. And I have fed them every single one of the recipes in these pages AND asked for their feedback. I've also fed these recipes to neighborhood children of varying ages who are neither gluten-free nor Paleo.

In this book you will find ZERO grain, gluten, dairy or refined sugar. And the majority of the recipes are also nut and egg free so that allergic children can indulge too. My goal is to bridge the gap between what kids love and what we'd actually love to feed them. So if you are ready to start, resume or finish that transition from the Standard American Diet to a grain-free, whole-foods based lifestyle, I'm here for you. I will hold your hand when you need it held and help make your kitchen a place that makes you proud.

From my family to yours, let's dig in!!

Tips for Transitioning

When I finally realized how much I needed to overhaul my own way of eating to help calm the effects of my autoimmune diseases and chronic infections like Lyme disease, I soon felt the unshakeable drive to shift my children's eating patterns and options. While I cannot say it is always a seamless transition, I do think there are ways to help sustain happy kids in the process. Here are a few tips that I think can really assist your family's clean food evolution.

1. Have a Backup Plan

If your kiddos have been accustomed to a Standard American Diet for years, giving up their favorite foods cold turkey is really tricky for some. Not to say that it can't be done, but as hard as it is for adults to make massive change, it can be even harder for kids, especially if they aren't young enough to be "fooled." If they are going to a party with pizza, ice cream and cake, or other off-limit foods, for example, make sure they have what they need to get their cravings covered and feel like they are part of the crowd. In the beginning feeling different can be difficult, so you'll want to make sure they feel special not isolated. I try to always carry snacks on me when we run errands too so that instead of a free cookie at the grocery store, I've got a snack readily available for when I've had to say no, which luckily becomes less and less as time goes on.

2. Don't Cave

As hard as it is, your kids need you to be the rock. Even when they are picky and fussy and make faces and refuse to eat, try not to cave! I offer one meal in my home for dinner. That's it. I refuse to spend time making custom meals. Is it hard sometimes? Yes. Does everyone like everything all the time? No. Do they have a choice? No. They do not have to clean their plates, but they have to try everything on it. If they want a small treat (sometimes just a teaspoon of soy/dairy-free chocolate chips), they are required to eat what I provide. I can assure you that my son, the eldest, is a very particular eater and always has been. He would forego all solids to just drink cow's milk, and eating real food was always a struggle. So it's not always easy. It's a commitment, and it takes time. If textures are an issue try pureeing, chopping, sautéing. Be more accommodating in the preparation, but don't trade out nutrients for snack foods. Some children are down to three or four preferred foods that are usually tan in color like chicken nuggets, pasta and grilled cheese. I've put those recipes in this book so that as you begin your transition. If they aren't ready for liver and zucchini noodles, they'll at least have options which are grain-, gluten- and dairy-free.

3. Recreate Favorites

Even after my kids were no longer eating gluten, they were still dependent on gluten-free mac 'n' cheese, pizza, noodles and so on for quite some time. Stocking rice noodles may have helped them avoid gluten, but it certainly didn't add in more greens! So when I secretly started Predominantly Paleo as a recipe-based blog, I needed to figure out how to make foods that were delicious enough that ANYONE would eat them! So I made all of the recipes in this book grain-, gluten-, dairy- and soy-free so they'd feel like they were getting their old favorites and I WOULD TOO! I also made the majority of them nut- and egg-free so that those with the top eight food allergies could indulge and feel "normal!" I find that if you recreate favorites in the beginning, that later on kids become a little more willing to try new things. My once gluten- and dairy-obsessed kids now fight over my Brussels sprouts. Don't worry, I've included that recipe in these pages!

4. Pack Lunches for School

If you send a child to school, there are MANY less than ideal choices in the cafeteria lines (at least in many schools). Our elementary school offers fresh veggies and fruits, but they also have lots of gluten- and dairy-laden options packed with less than desirable ingredients. So I have packed my kids' lunches from day one. They do not get cookies in their lunches. I do shoot to get at least one colorful veggie in there a day. Now that I trust them to make good decisions, they are allowed to choose a side from the cafeteria line, which they think is a privilege. They choose options like raw fresh vegetables or even bottled water instead of white dinner rolls you could use to shatter windows. This wasn't always the case, however. It is a process and one that takes perseverance. In this book, I've included some sample lunches so that if you feel uninspired or lost as to what to provide instead of cheese crackers, I'll help show you some options which are delicious and also nutrient dense!

5. Educate

Unfortunately my kids have witnessed my illness at its very worst. While we naturally want to protect our children from the evils of the world, I do use my decline as a teaching tool. We often talk about how treating our bodies right and feeding them healthy foods can help prevent disease or help provide support to a body that is having a hard time. They know that if they eat fast food and other processed low-quality foods that they could potentially end up sick. Find examples to show them how good foods can benefit us. Show them the perimeter of the grocery store, how to pick produce, why pasture raised animals can be healthier animals to consume than conventionally raised ones. Each trip to the grocery or farmers' markets is an opportunity to teach lessons of why we choose healthy foods and what their powers are in our bodies.

6. Get Them Involved

Kids who are involved can experience a lot more enthusiasm about healthy eating. Let them help meal plan for the week by having them tell you what recipes they've really liked in the past. Buy a set of kid-friendly knives and let them help cook! Kids typically love to feel useful and also love spending time with us (until they hit their tweens!), so take advantage of the extra hands even when it means exercising a little extra patience. Also keep good quality snacks available to pack their lunches—I keep mine where they can reach so that they can help fill their own lunchboxes in the morning. I believe autonomy and good decision making backed with positive reinforcement and praise helps encourage more of the same. Additionally, when we get a new cookbook, I give them each a specific color of adhesive page tabs to pick the recipes they'd like to try. They LOVE flipping through pretty pictures and finding delicious eats, and even the little kiddos can do this! Oh, and take them to a farmer's market—let them pick out a new item of produce they've never tried before. It can be a fun activity that also turns into an opportunity to introduce new foods!

7. Make it Fun

If your kids are really young you can have fun with food! We used to call broccoli "little trees" and pretend to be giants or dinosaurs eating them. Mealtime shouldn't have to be parents screaming at kids to eat their healthy foods. This never ends well, as many of you may know. Making mealtime more lighthearted and fun can encourage kids to eat and try new foods without it being a chore or a punishment. You can also take it outside and make it a picnic or eat at the park. Sometimes a change of venue can be uplifting and allow for more exploration.

8. Positive Reinforcement

Celebrate your child's good choices. They seek our approval and want us to be proud of them. Sometimes positive reinforcement of eating their baby spinach can be a lot more encouraging than punishing them for not doing so. I went through a phase where dinner often meant me raising my voice and sending kids to their rooms. In the end, I never got what I wanted, and my kids didn't benefit either. Now I always try to let them know they have a choice and praise them for making the right choice. Dinners have become much more pleasant and less combative.

9. Maintain a No Junk Kitchen

If you have a cupboard stocked with cookies and snack cakes, your challenge will be that much greater, especially with older kids. Don't even let the junk be an option. Now with that said, if there is a gluten-free bakery or a unique restaurant outside the home where you can occasionally celebrate a birthday or special event, it can always be reserved for just that. But by keeping the garbage out of your house, it won't be a temptation. I learned long ago that if it made it into my shopping cart, it would most certainly find its way to my mouth. So leave it at the store!

10. Be the Change

It is virtually impossible to get your family on board if you are sporting a 72-ounce (2.1 L) soda from your local convenience store. Show them how it's done by setting an example. Snacking on veggies instead of a fistful of Halloween candy will make you much more accountable and respected when it comes to the kids making their own choices.

11. Be Sneaky

Yes, you read that right—become stealthy like a superhero. If you are struggling to get kids on board in the beginning, sneak the nutrients into them. There are many opportunities in these recipes to sneak in extra greens, gelatin and nutrients. Many veggies puree easily and can be added into baked goods. So if your picky-pants eater isn't ready to dive face first into a bowl of collard greens, that's OK. Find some opportunities to get the good stuff into them anyway. Get creative!

Good Morning, Sunshine

It's no secret that starting your child's day with a nutrient-packed meal increases energy and helps them focus once they are school aged. If your little one is a picky eater, this can cause many challenges. And if your child's diet is further complicated by food allergies or intolerances, meals can become that much more frustrating for you!

In this breakfast chapter, I've pulled together a selection of ways to start the day. All of them are made without grain, gluten, dairy, soy and refined sugar. I've also included an assortment of recipes without nuts or eggs in case those are off the menu. With recipes like classic French Toast Sticks (page 26), Allergy-Friendly Waffles (page 18), Grain- + Nut-Free Granola (page 22) and Green Eggs + Ham Roll Ups (page 38), you can honor your child's body and also make the stuff kids really want!

Allergy-Friendly Waffles

GRAIN FREE, GLUTEN FREE, DAIRY FREE, NUT FREE, EGG FREE, SOY FREE

How in the world is it possible to make waffles for your littles when they need to avoid grain, gluten, dairy, eggs AND nuts?! It feels impossible, but it's not anymore! This recipe is completely allergy-friendly, yet embodies all the crispy perfection that waffles should have.

MAKES: 2 SERVINGS

⅓ cup (40 g) tapioca starch

⅓ cup (50 g) potato starch

3 tbsp (18 g) coconut flour

¼ cup (60 g) sustainable palm shortening, melted

3 tbsp (45 ml) 100% maple syrup

⅔ cup (160 ml) coconut milk

Pinch salt

½ tsp baking soda

Cooking fat for greasing waffle iron

Dairy-Free Butter (page 194)

100% maple syrup or local honey

Preheat a standard (not Belgian) waffle iron. Keep in mind that the serving size of this recipe will vary based on how much batter is required to fill your waffle iron.

Mix all of the ingredients in a mixing bowl, stirring by hand to remove the lumps. Once the waffle iron is heated, be sure to grease it thoroughly. If not well oiled, your waffles can split apart when opening the iron.

Spoon batter into the iron, leaving room for it to spread while cooking. Allow the waffle to cook until your iron indicates it is cooked through, then carefully open your waffle iron and remove the crispy waffle with a fork. Repeat with remaining batter.

Serve with my Dairy-Free Butter and 100% maple syrup or honey.

FOR LITTLE HANDS: Allow your child to help mix all the ingredients together and stir. Older helpers may also spoon the batter into the waffle iron while supervised.

Egg in a Hole

GRAIN FREE, GLUTEN FREE, DAIRY FREE, NUT FREE, SOY FREE

This old classic is loved by kids and grown ups alike and is often a first recipe learned in the kitchen. With my Legit Sandwich Bread recipe (page 148) it can enter your kitchen once again with that toasty house for your sunny morning egg! Don't forget to soak up the yummy yellow with a bite of warm comforting buttery toast!

MAKES: 4 SERVINGS

4 slices Legit Sandwich Bread (page 148)

Ghee, Dairy-Free Butter (page 194) or cooking fat of choice

4 eggs

Sea salt to taste

Ground black pepper to taste

You have two options for cooking up this recipe: either baking or frying.

To bake, preheat the oven to 350°F (175°C). Take one slice of bread and cut out a hole. You may choose to do this with a cookie cutter of any design so long as it does not cut into the outside borders of the bread slice as this is what holds the egg in place.

Place the bread on a parchment-lined baking sheet. Crack the egg into the hole in the center of the bread slice. Sprinkle with salt and pepper. Take the bread cut out and spread it with the cooking fat. Place it alongside the egg-filled bread and repeat with the remaining eggs and bread slices. Bake for up to 10 minutes, or until the white is cooked through and the yolk is still runny. Remove baking sheet from oven and serve.

To cook in a skillet or on a griddle, heat a greased skillet or griddle to medium-high. Take one slice of bread and cut out a hole. You may choose to do this with a cookie cutter of any design so long as it does not cut into the outside borders of the bread slice. This is what holds the egg in place. Place the bread slice into the skillet or griddle and crack an egg into the cut out. You have two options here: either cover your egg-filled toasts and allow the whites to cook through for about 4 minutes, or you can cook just until the whites set underneath (about a minute) and then flip the toast over to cook the other side (about 2 to 3 more minutes). Covering the egg-filled toasts without flipping will yield more of a sunny-side-up egg; if you flip them, they will yield more of a fried egg with a runny yolk. To cook the yolk through, simply cook for longer. While the egg filled-toasts cook, grease the cut outs and toast them alongside the larger toasts, flipping once the underneath side is toasted.

 FOR LITTLE HANDS: Allow your little one to help butter the toasts, help crack the eggs into the toasts or, if older, help flip the toasts on the griddle, paying close attention to the hot surface.

Grain- + Nut-Free Granola

GRAIN FREE, GLUTEN FREE, DAIRY FREE, NUT FREE, EGG FREE, SOY FREE

The great thing about grain-free eating is the versatility and magic of nuts behaving as grains. But sadly those with nut allergies become limited once more. I wanted to create a granola that was just as good in yogurt and in milk as it is alone as a quick snack. This one is both grain and nut free and is packed with lots of nutrients that both little kids and grown kids will love!

MAKES: 6 SERVINGS

1 cup (140 g) sunflower seeds
½ cup (59 g) toasted pumpkin seeds
¼ cup (42 g) flax seeds
½ cup (85 g) unsweetened flaked coconut
½ cup (93 g) unsweetened shredded coconut
2 tbsp (12 g) coconut flour
2 tbsp (14 g) sweet potato flour
¼ cup (60 ml) local honey
2 tbsp (17 g) sunflower seed butter
½ cup (112 g) dairy- and soy-free chocolate chips

Preheat the oven to 350°F (175°C) and line a large baking sheet with parchment paper.

Combine all the ingredients in a mixing bowl and then spread them out on the baking sheet.

Bake for 10 minutes, then redistribute the contents and bake for another 5 to 10 minutes, being careful not to burn.

Remove the baking sheet from the oven. Allow the granola to cool, then store in an air-tight container at room temperature.

 FOR LITTLE HANDS: Allow your child to mix all of the ingredients by hand and then spread the mixture out onto the parchment-lined baking sheet. They can also help break the baked mixture apart into smaller clusters once it has cooled. Older kids may be able to complete the recipe start to finish with some supervision.

Fruit Kabobs + Dairy-Free Dip

GRAIN FREE, GLUTEN FREE, DAIRY FREE, NUT FREE, EGG FREE, SOY FREE

Have you ever noticed that children are drawn to vibrantly colored foods, often artificial? Keep the colors from nature available to them with these fruit kabobs and tasty dairy-free dip! It's the perfect allergy-friendly breakfast that is as beautiful as it is tasty!

MAKES: 4 SERVINGS

1 (13½ ounce [370 ml]) can full-fat coconut milk, refrigerated for at least 2 hours

1 tbsp (15 ml) honey

¼ tsp pure vanilla extract

½ tsp orange or mandarin zest

3-4 cups (500-650 g) chopped fruit (strawberries, raspberries, cantaloupe, pineapple, honeydew, blueberries, blackberries)

Begin by opening the coconut milk and carefully spooning out the coconut cream, which has settled at the top, into a mixing bowl. Once you get down to the liquid milk part of the can, stop spooning, as this part will change the consistency of your dip, making it less whipped.

Add in honey, vanilla extract and orange zest. Using a whisk or hand mixer, beat the mixture until it is well combined and fluffy like whipped cream. Set the dip aside.

Slide the fruits onto bamboo skewers. I chose to make mine in a rainbow so that they were extra inviting to the kids!

 FOR LITTLE HANDS: Allow your child to help whisk the coconut cream or to help skewer the fruit. If your child is younger, you might even throw in a color lesson—why not?

French Toast Sticks

GRAIN FREE, GLUTEN FREE, DAIRY FREE, NUT FREE, SOY FREE

It is virtually impossible for both little kids and big kids not to fall in love with these French Toast Sticks. The sweet, filling, finger food nature makes them a crowd pleaser for nearly everyone. This recipe begins with my Legit Sandwich Bread (page 148) and ends in paradise...breakfast paradise that is!

MAKES: 4 SERVINGS

1 loaf Legit Sandwich Bread (page 148)

4 eggs

½ cup (120 ml) full-fat coconut milk

1 tsp ground cinnamon

2 tbsp (30 ml) pure maple syrup, plus extra for serving

¼ tsp ground nutmeg

1 tsp vanilla extract

2 tbsp (30 g) ghee, avocado oil or coconut oil

Optional: tapioca starch for dusting

Slice the bread into sandwich slices and then each slice into 4 to 5 sticks.

In a medium-sized mixing bowl, combine the eggs, coconut milk, cinnamon, maple syrup, nutmeg and vanilla. Whisk until well combined.

Heat the cooking fat in a medium sized skillet over medium/high heat. While that heats, submerge about one-fourth of the bread sticks into the egg mixture.

After about 30 seconds, making sure they are coated well, remove the bread sticks and transfer them to the skillet. Cook on both sides for about 2 to 3 minutes per side, then transfer them once more to a plate. Repeat with remaining bread sticks until all of your French toast is cooked. Serve with additional maple syrup or fresh fruit. You may also dust them with tapioca starch to create a "powdered sugar" appeal.

 FOR LITTLE HANDS: Allow your helper to cut the bread with a kid-friendly knife and whisk together the egg mixture. Your child can also submerge the bread sticks in the egg mixture. Older children can cook the French toast sticks in the skillet while supervised.

Sausage Quiche

GRAIN FREE, GLUTEN FREE, DAIRY FREE, NUT FREE, SOY FREE

Eggs, for those who tolerate them, are a fantastic source of nutrients. But sometimes it's nice to switch it up a bit and not serve them out of a skillet every time. This quiche recipe is one I've regularly made for my family for dinner, and they adore it! The savory garlic and onion pack this quiche with aromatics and the sausage helps give it that hearty, stick-to-your-ribs goodness for lots of energy to start the day!

MAKES: 6 SERVINGS

FOR THE CRUST
1 cup (128 g) cassava flour
¼ cup (60 g) palm shortening, melted
2 tbsp (30 ml) dairy-free milk like flax, coconut or almond (use more if needed)
Pinch sea salt
1 pastured egg

FOR THE FILLING
6 ounces (168 g) pasture raised breakfast sausage, cooked
4 eggs
¼ cup (60 ml) dairy-free milk like flax, coconut or almond
¼ tsp garlic powder
¼ tsp onion powder
½ onion diced
½ tsp sea salt
Optional: 2 tbsp (2 g) chopped cilantro

Preheat the oven to 350°F (175°C).

Combine the crust ingredients in a mixing bowl and use your hands to combine them well. Press the crust dough into the center and up the sides of a greased pie tin. If you prefer a thicker crust you can slightly increase the cassava flour and fat to create more dough. Slide the pie tin into the oven and bake for 10 minutes.

While the crust is baking, combine the quiche filling ingredients in another mixing bowl and whisk to combine. Once the crust is finished baking, remove it and pour the egg mixture into the center. Bake for 30 minutes or until the center is baked through. Remove, slice and serve.

FOR LITTLE HANDS: Allow your child to mix the crust ingredients by hand. Many children enjoy the tactile nature of working the dough. Your helper may also help whisk the filling ingredients and pour the mixture into the baked crust.

Cinnamon Maple Plantains

GRAIN FREE, GLUTEN FREE, DAIRY FREE, NUT FREE, EGG FREE, SOY FREE

Finding allergy-friendly breakfast foods can be a real challenge sometimes. Now make those foods kid-friendly too, and you've got your hands full. These Cinnamon Maple Plantains are warm and comforting, slightly sweet and made with good fats for your little one. So when eggs are out, plantains are in—and they'll start your munchkin off with all the right stuff.

MAKES: 2 SERVINGS

2 ripe plantains
1–2 tbsp (15–30 g) ghee, avocado, olive or coconut oil
½ tsp ground cinnamon
2 tbsp (30 ml) maple syrup

To peel the plantains, slice off the ends and then make a lengthwise slice through the skin, making it easier to remove. Once the plantains are peeled, slice into ⅛-inch (3-mm) thick discs.

Heat the cooking fat in a large skillet over medium/high heat. Once hot, place the plantain slices in the hot oil and sprinkle evenly with half the cinnamon. Once the underneath side of the slices starts to brown slightly, after around 4 to 5 minutes, carefully turn them over. Sprinkle with the remaining cinnamon and drizzle evenly with the maple syrup. Allow them to continue browning until slightly crispy and then remove from heat and cooking fat. Serve warm.

 FOR LITTLE HANDS: Using a kid-safe knife, you can allow your child to help slice the plantains.

Silver Dollar Chocolate Chip Pancakes

GRAIN FREE, GLUTEN FREE, DAIRY FREE, NUT FREE, SOY FREE

Growing up, our special treat as kids was to get homemade chocolate chip pancakes on the weekends. Back then, gluten and dairy were of no consequence, so we enjoyed every last bite thoroughly. Fast forward to recent times when I wanted to recreate a childhood favorite of my own for my children, but needed a better way. When I make these, they scramble over the last one and have been known to get pretty competitive in doing so! Make a double batch I say!

MAKES: 2 SERVINGS

2 eggs

¼ cup (24 g) coconut flour

¼ cup (30 g) tapioca starch

⅓ cup (80 ml) coconut milk, flax milk or other dairy-free milk

½ tsp baking soda

1 tbsp (15 g) coconut oil, melted

1 tbsp (15 ml) 100% maple syrup

Pinch sea salt

½ cup soy- and dairy-free chocolate chips (or more to taste)

Extra coconut oil, ghee or preferred fat for cooking

Coconut Whipped Cream (page 197)

Preheat a griddle or large skillet over medium/high heat with about a tablespoon (15 g) of oil.

Combine all of the pancake ingredients in a bowl except for the chocolate chips and stir, whisk or blend with a stick blender until the batter is smooth. Add in the chocolate chips and stir once more to combine.

Spoon the pancake batter into the hot skillet, spacing the pancakes at least 2 inches (5 cm) apart. Cook the pancakes until they begin to bubble, about 2 to 3 minutes and then flip them to the alternate side for another few minutes. Remove the cooked pancakes from the skillet or griddle and serve them with coconut whipped cream and a few extra chocolate chips if desired.

FOR LITTLE HANDS: Allow your child to help mix the pancake ingredients in a bowl. Older children may also help flip the pancakes on the griddle while supervised.

Pale-O's Cereal

GRAIN FREE, GLUTEN FREE, DAIRY FREE, NUT FREE, EGG FREE, SOY FREE

I hear a lot from people of all ages who say that when they give up grain they really miss a bowl of cereal for breakfast. I can't say that I blame them, and it's even harder being a kid without that morning bowl of happy. I created this recipe so that a bowl of cereal is not out of the question after giving up grains AND so that there could be a better option for finger foods for the littlest eaters. I recommend making a big batch and storing in the freezer so that you'll always have it available!

MAKES: 3 SERVINGS

⅓ cup (32 g) coconut flour
⅓ cup (42 g) cassava flour
⅓ cup (80 g) coconut oil
1 tsp 100% vanilla extract
3 tbsp (45 ml) 100% maple syrup
¼ cup (60 ml) coconut milk
Pinch sea salt

Preheat the oven to 350°F (175°C).

Combine all ingredients in a bowl. The dough should be thick, but able to be piped. Once desired consistency is reached, spoon mixture into a sandwich bag or piping bag. Cut a small tip off the corner of the sandwich bag. On a parchment-lined baking sheet, pipe small dollops of dough, about ⅓ inch (7 mm) in diameter (or to your size preference). Bake for around 10 to 12 minutes, depending on your oven, then remove and allow to cool. The nuggets should be nicely browned and will crisp more upon cooling, after about 5 minutes or so. Many kids love these as a fun finger food versus a cereal to submerge in milk, but they are delicious however you decide to serve them!

 FOR LITTLE HANDS: Allow your child to help mix the dough ingredients and help pipe the cereal if your helper is a little older.

Green Eggs + Ham Roll Ups

GRAIN FREE, GLUTEN FREE, DAIRY FREE, NUT FREE, SOY FREE

This one is a classic in a book, in a kitchen, on a table, in a mouth...well, you get it. Pack in good greens instead of food coloring to make this favorite book into a favorite breakfast meal.

MAKES: 3 ROLL UPS

1–2 tbsp (15–30 g) ghee, avocado, olive or coconut oil

3 eggs

½ cup (or more) (15 g) baby spinach leaves

Sea salt and/or ground black pepper to taste

3 slices of pastured/organic ham lunchmeat slices

In a small or medium-sized skillet, heat the cooking fat over medium heat.

While the fat warms, crack the eggs into a blender and add the baby spinach. Blend on high until the spinach is completely blended into the eggs, around a minute or two.

Pour the blended spinach and egg mixture into the skillet and cook over medium heat, shifting them regularly until they are cooked through, around 5 minutes. Season with sea salt and/or pepper.

Spoon one-third of the green eggs into the center of a slice of ham. Wrap the ham around the eggs and if necessary secure them with a blunt edged toothpick. Repeat with the remaining eggs, distributed between the last two slices of ham. Serve warm.

 FOR LITTLE HANDS: While supervised, you may allow your little one to crack the eggs, help operate the blender and even shift the eggs in the skillet. Kids love power tools and this is a great opportunity to teach safety in the kitchen!

Main Squeeze

Sometimes dinnertime is filled with struggles and frustrations, yelling and threatening. This is no way to spend a family meal and certainly doesn't accomplish what we hope to during our time together.

Unfortunately, some kids are really particular when it comes to their favorite foods and their willingness to venture out to new textures and flavors. While this can be very normal, it's also not what we want for our children in terms of long-term nutrition.

The recipes in this chapter recreate all of your child's favorites like Chicken Nuggets (page 49), Grilled "Cheese" (page 53) and even Crispy Sweet Potato Fish Sticks (page 46) the whole family will love. What's even better is these recipes are made with the highest quality, least inflammatory ingredients so you can give your family the foods they crave, but you know that the grain, gluten, dairy, soy and refined sugars won't be there.

I like to think of these recipes as the gateway to nutrient-dense foods, so if your children aren't there quite yet, they will be soon enough!

Glazed Grain-Free Meatloaf + Crispy Onion Topping

GRAIN FREE, GLUTEN FREE, DAIRY FREE, NUT FREE, EGG FREE, SOY FREE

I'll be the first to admit that I am a huge meatloaf fan and so are my children. But meatloaf is one of those one-pot-wonders that doesn't appeal to little ones with resistant-to-try attitudes. This loaf, however, is topped with a sweet and tangy tomato glaze and crispy fried onions that quite honestly create a family favorite almost anyone will love!

MAKES: 6 SERVINGS

FOR THE MEATLOAF

2 pounds (910 g) grass fed organic ground beef

2 tsp (6 g) onion powder

2 tsp (6 g) garlic powder

1 tsp sea salt

1 tsp ground pepper

¼ cup (60 ml) Ketchup (page 174) or high-quality store-bought

¼ cup (60 ml) dairy-free milk (coconut, flax, almond)

FOR THE GLAZE

½ cup (120 ml) Ketchup (page 174) or high-quality store-bought

1 tbsp (15 ml) pure maple syrup

1 tbsp (12 g) coconut sugar

1 tbsp (15 ml) apple cider vinegar

FOR THE CRISPY ONIONS

1 large onion, thinly sliced

½ cup (120 ml) full fat coconut milk (or preferred dairy-free milk)

½ cup (60 g) tapioca flour

3 tbsp (18 g) coconut flour

½ tsp garlic sea salt

Avocado oil, coconut oil, ghee or olive oil for frying

You can pressure cook or bake this meatloaf, depending on the time you have and which equipment.

To make in a pressure cooker, combine all the meatloaf ingredients into a loaf and wrap in foil. Pressure cook on high for about 35 minutes and then quick release the pressure.

To bake the meatloaf, preheat oven to 375°F (190°C). Now combine all ingredients and form them into a loaf. Place it in a loaf pan and bake for 45 minutes to an hour or until cooked through.

While the meatloaf is cooking, prepare the glaze by combining the ketchup, maple syrup, coconut sugar and vinegar in a small saucepan over medium heat. Stir occasionally for about 5 to 8 minutes and set aside.

Prepare the onions for frying by pouring the dairy-free milk onto one clean plate and mixing the two flours and salt on another. (You may use 1 cup [128 g] of cassava flour for dredging in place of the coconut and tapioca flour combination.) Preheat the cooking fat over medium/high heat in a large skillet. Submerge the onions in the milk and then dredge them in the flour mixture. Fry them in batches until all of the onions are cooked and crispy.

Once the meatloaf is finished cooking, spoon the glaze over the top and sprinkle the crispy fried onions over the glaze. Slice and serve warm.

 FOR LITTLE HANDS: Allow your child to help mix all the meatloaf ingredients together and form the loaf. Older helpers can help dredge and fry the onions as well.

Veggie Spaghetti + Meatballs

GRAIN FREE, GLUTEN FREE, DAIRY FREE, NUT FREE, EGG FREE, SOY FREE

Spaghetti and meatballs is the tried and true winner of children's hearts everywhere! Ever wonder how to transition this one to a healthier dish? The secret's in the noodle swap! The fun part about noodles is not the inflammatory gluten; it's their slurpability. That's a word right?! By making veggie noodles from squash, your family can slurp with the best of them and be gaining tons of micronutrients at the same time! Winner, winner spaghetti dinner!

MAKES: 4 SERVINGS

1 (24 ounce [710 ml]) jar organic marinara sauce, divided

1 pound (455 g) grass-fed ground beef

1 tsp onion powder

1 tsp garlic powder

½ tsp ground black pepper

3-4 tbsp (24-32 g) tapioca starch

¼ cup (60 ml) full-fat coconut milk (optional)

3 large zucchini or yellow squash, spiral cut

2-3 tbsp (30-45 g) ghee, avocado oil or preferred cooking fat

Preheat the oven to 350°F (175°C).

In a mixing bowl, combine 3 to 4 tablespoons (45 to 60 ml) of the marinara sauce, the beef, onion powder, garlic powder, black pepper and tapioca starch. Mix well by hand, incorporating all ingredients. Form the meatballs by taking a large tablespoon of the meat mixture and rolling into a ball. Repeat with the remaining meat mixture.

Place the uncooked meatballs onto a parchment-lined baking sheet and bake for 15 to 20 minutes or until cooked through and no longer pink in the center.

In large deep skillet, combine the remaining marinara sauce and the coconut milk over medium/high heat, until it begins to simmer, around 5 minutes. Add the baked meatballs to the sauce and allow to simmer while you prepare the noodles.

In another large deep skillet, heat the cooking fat on high. Cook the spiral cut squash in the hot fat until tender, about 5 to 8 minutes, or longer if you prefer very soft noodles. Remove noodles from skillet, leaving behind any water that has cooked off of the vegetables.

Serve noodles warm with meatballs and sauce.

 FOR LITTLE HANDS: Let your child help with spiral cutting the squash (supervised) or with helping mix and shape the meatballs.

Crispy Sweet Potato Fish Sticks

GRAIN FREE, GLUTEN FREE, DAIRY FREE, NUT FREE, EGG FREE, SOY FREE

I've taken that favorite finger food and made them allergy friendly by creating an egg-free, grain-free crust out of sweet potato chips! Your little dunker will love dipping these and you can be confident that all of the ingredients are safe! Try my Honey Mustard (page 170), Ranch Dressing (page 173) or Awesome Sauce (page 177) as dips.

MAKES: 4 SERVINGS

4 ounces (112 g) crushed sweet potato chips (fried in avocado, olive or coconut oil)

⅓ cup (42 g) tapioca starch

1 tsp garlic sea salt

¼ cup (60 g) avocado, olive or coconut oil, ghee or sustainable palm shortening

¾ pound (340 g) wild caught cod (or other white fish)

Preheat the oven to 350°F (175°C).

On a clean plate, combine the sweet potato chips, tapioca starch and garlic sea salt.

Preheat the frying oil in a large skillet over medium/high heat.

Slice your fish into sticks and dredge them in the breading mixture. If your breading isn't sticking well, mash the chips smaller and use your fingers to press the breading onto the fish. Fry the coated fish sticks in small batches, flipping them after a minute or so on each side. You'll want to crisp them up a bit before removing them.

Once the fish sticks have been fried briefly, transfer them to a baking rack placed atop a baking sheet. This will help excess oil drain off while your fish sticks continue to cook in the oven.

Bake the fish sticks for around 20 minutes. Remove and serve warm with your favorite dipping sauce.

 FOR LITTLE HANDS: Allow your child to help smash the chips into crumbs, combine the crust ingredients on a plate and dredge the fish sticks to coat them. Older children may help fry the fish sticks while supervised as well.

Chicken Nuggets

GRAIN FREE, GLUTEN FREE, DAIRY FREE, NUT FREE, EGG FREE, SOY FREE

If ever there was a quintessential kids' food, this is it. And it's no coincidence that it is the hardest to give up for many. I've created these nuggets to have the texture of the more processed ones, but have made them with organic pasture raised chicken, and omitted grain, gluten, dairy, egg, nuts and soy-based ingredients.

MAKES: 3-4 SERVINGS

1 pound (455 g) chicken breast (organic, pasture raised preferred)

1 tsp sea salt, divided

1 tsp onion powder, divided

1 tsp garlic powder, divided

1 tsp ground black pepper, divided

Avocado oil, coconut oil, ghee or lard for frying

¼ cup (30 g) tapioca starch

2 tbsp (12 g) coconut flour

¼ cup (40 g) potato starch

½ cup (120 ml) full-fat coconut milk

Preheat the oven to 350°F (175°C).

Sprinkle chicken breasts with ½ teaspoon each salt, onion powder, garlic powder and pepper. Cook the chicken breasts by either baking them at 350°F (175°C) for about 25 to 30 minutes or until cooked through or pressure cooking for 15 minutes.

Once the chicken breasts are cooked through, chop into pieces and then blend them using a traditional blender or food processor. Blending the chicken helps create the smoother, more uniform texture preferred by picky eaters.

Heat the cooking fat over medium/high heat. The fat must be hot enough to ensure the nuggets will crisp.

Mix the tapioca, coconut flour, potato starch and remaining seasonings on one clean plate, and pour the coconut milk onto another clean plate.

Take about a tablespoon (15 g) of the blended chicken and form it into a nugget shape. Saturate both sides of the nugget in the milk then dredge it in the flour mixture. Repeat these two steps to double-coat the nuggets before frying. Once your oil is hot enough, begin the frying process.

You only need to fry on both sides of the nuggets until they are crispy enough to serve, since the chicken has been cooked through prior to this point. Once the nuggets are crispy and nicely browned, remove them with a skimmer or slotted spatula and place them on a towel-lined plate. You will want to serve these right away (making certain they are not too hot of course) for optimal texture. They will become less crisp if left to sit too long.

 FOR LITTLE HANDS: Let your child help dredge the nuggets in the flour or even help shape the nuggets. Because some younger children are turned off by meat, they may find that participating helps take out the yuck factor.

Mini Pizzas

GRAIN FREE, GLUTEN FREE, DAIRY FREE, EGG FREE, SOY FREE

It's quite tragic that this absolutely adored favorite kid food be 100% laden with dairy and gluten. So it was a complete no-brainer that I needed to recreate it, not only for pizza loving kids everywhere but for grown-ups too!!!

MAKES: 4 SERVINGS

FOR THE CHEESE
1 cup (140 g) cashews
½ tsp apple cider vinegar
¾ tsp garlic sea salt
2 heaping tsp (10 g) nutritional yeast
¼ cup (32 g) tapioca flour
1 cup (240 ml) hot water

FOR THE CRUST
¾ cup (96 g) cassava flour
¼ cup (32 g) arrowroot or tapioca flour
1 tbsp (6 g) coconut flour
1 tbsp (12 g) coconut sugar
½ tsp baking soda
½ tsp garlic sea salt
¼ cup (60 g) ghee or avocado oil
½ cup (120 ml) dairy-free milk
1 tbsp (7 g) ground flax seed

FOR THE SAUCE
1 (14½ ounce [400 g]) can petite diced tomatoes
1 tsp dried basil
½ tsp dried oregano
1 tbsp (15 ml) pure maple syrup
1 tbsp (12 g) maple sugar
1 tbsp (15 ml) olive oil
½ tsp or more sea salt
¼ tsp ground black pepper
½ tsp onion powder
1 tsp garlic powder
1 tsp dried parsley

To make the cheese, soak your cashews in water for at least an hour. Then drain the cashews and place them in a blender with all the other cheese ingredients. Blend on high for a solid 2 minutes. You want the consistency to be perfectly creamy AND you want the tapioca to help thicken the cheese mixture. After 2 minutes of blending, pour the cheese into a bowl and place in the fridge or freezer while you make the crust.

Preheat the oven to 350°F (175°C).

Combine all crust ingredients in a bowl and knead by hand until you have a big ball of dough. Divide the dough into 4 equal sized balls. Roll out the dough between two pieces of parchment paper to desired thickness. If your dough cracks around the edges, just seal it back together by hand. I recommend making a thin crust with this one for optimal results.

Bake the crusts for 8 to 10 minutes on each side, for a total of 16 to 20 minutes.

To make the pizza sauce, combine all of the ingredients in a blender and puree until you smooth. You can use it right away, uncooked, or heat it on low in a saucepan.

Remove the baked crusts and spoon pizza sauce on top followed by whatever veggie/meat toppings you prefer. Remove the cheese from the fridge or freezer and spoon/drizzle it over the toppings. You can spoon it liberally, but it can be quite liquid. This is normal!

Return the pizzas to the oven and turn on your broiler for 5 minutes OR LESS!

You want the cheese to begin to solidify and even begin to brown, but you do not want to burn your crust or toppings.

FOR LITTLE HANDS: Your little one can help by adding the ingredients to the mixing bowl and combining them by hand. Your helper can also roll out the dough or decorate the pizzas with desired toppings! Older helpers can also make the cashew cheese using the blender, while supervised.

Grilled "Cheese"

GRAIN FREE, GLUTEN FREE, DAIRY FREE, SOY FREE

Pull up a bowl of tomato soup, because this party is about to get started. My Legit Sandwich Bread (page 148) mimics real gluten-based bread so well, you can even grill it! And you'd never guess my "cheese" doesn't have a bit of dairy in it with its creamy, gooey, meltiness! A happy day for us all!

MAKES: 5 SERVINGS

1 cup (140 g) raw, soaked cashews

½ cup (120 ml) water, divided

¼ cup (15 g) nutritional yeast

½ tsp onion powder

½ tsp garlic powder

Pinch paprika (you can use smoked also)

1 tsp sea salt

2 tsp (10 g) pimentos (without liquid)

Squeeze of fresh lemon juice (to taste, you can use more if desired)

1 tbsp (7 g) grass-fed gelatin (use 1½ tbsp [11 g] for firmer)

1 loaf Legit Sandwich Bread (page 148)

1–2 tbsp (15–30 g) ghee, sustainable palm shortening or preferred fat

NUT-FREE "CHEESE" OPTION

1 cup (240 ml) dairy-free milk

¼ cup (15 g) nutritional yeast

½ tsp onion powder

½ tsp garlic powder

1 tsp sea salt

2 tbsp (30 g) ghee

Paprika to taste (and color)

1 tbsp (10 g) pimentos

¼ cup (15 g) tapioca starch

3 tbsp (45 g) grass-fed gelatin

Soak the cashews for 4 hours or more. In a blender, combine the drained, soaked cashews, ¼ cup (60 ml) water, nutritional yeast, onion powder, garlic powder, paprika, sea salt, pimentos and lemon juice. Blend on high until creamy. If you have a hard time getting a smooth consistency, add a tiny bit of water at a time and scrape the edges of the blender until this is achieved. You'll want it to be as creamy as possible. Spoon the blended mixture into a small saucepan and heat over low/medium heat, stirring regularly.

In a small bowl, combine the gelatin and the remaining ¼ cup (60 ml) water. Stir very well to combine, then quickly incorporate it into the saucepan mixture. Stir until all the water is incorporated completely then remove the saucepan from heat and pour the mixture into a parchment-lined container—a glass bowl, loaf pan, really anything that you'd like to use so long as it is smallish. You want the cheese to be as deep as possible once poured in.

Refrigerate for an hour or two until the cheese firms up.

Slice the loaf of Legit Sandwich Bread into 10 slices. Remove the cheese from the refrigerator and slice. Heat 1 to 2 teaspoons (5 to 10 g) of the cooking fat in a large skillet over medium/high heat. Assemble one sandwich at a time and then grill it on both sides until the cheese is melted and the bread toasted, about 1 minute or so per side. Continue with remaining sandwiches.

For the nut-free cheese option, combine all ingredients, except the gelatin, in a blender and puree. Pour the mixture into a saucepan and heat on medium heat. Whisk in the gelatin for 1 minute and then transfer the mixture back to the blender and puree once more. The mixture should be thicker than before. Pour into a container and refrigerate to set, up to an hour. Slice and serve on grilled cheese, following the instructions above.

 FOR LITTLE HANDS: Allow your child to help mix the cheese ingredients in the blender while supervised. Or help slice the bread with a kid-friendly knife and assemble the sandwiches.

Chicken Zoodle Soup

GRAIN FREE, GLUTEN FREE, DAIRY FREE, NUT FREE, EGG FREE, SOY FREE

I am pretty sure it is illegal to be a kiddo and not like chicken noodle soup. This one has gut-healing broth paired with veggie noodles for a complete meal that is perfect for slurping! You can choose to cook on the stovetop, with a pressure cooker or with a slow cooker.

MAKES: 4 SERVINGS

32 ounces (950 ml) Chicken Bone Broth (page 72) or high-quality store-bought

1 pound (455 g) boneless chicken breast, diced

1 cup (128 g) carrots, diced

½ cup (50 g) celery, diced

1 onion, diced

¼ tsp ground black pepper

½ tsp sea salt

½ tsp garlic powder

½ tsp onion powder

1–2 zucchini or yellow squash

1 tbsp (15 g) avocado oil, olive oil or ghee

To make on the stovetop, place all ingredients except for the squash and cooking fat in a stockpot and turn the heat on high. Once it begins to boil, turn down heat to a simmer and cook for about 35 minutes or until the chicken is cooked through and the veggies are softened.

To make this in a pressure cooker or Instant Pot, place all ingredients, except for the squash and cooking fat, into your cooker and secure the lid. Bring up to pressure for 25 minutes then quickly release the pressure.

To make in a slow cooker, place all contents in the slow cooker except for the squash and cooking fat. Cook on low for 6 hours or 3 to 4 hours on high.

Follow the remaining instructions below.

While the soup is cooking, spiral cut or julienne the squash to make noodles. Sauté in the cooking fat over medium high heat until softened, around 8 minutes. If you prefer them more al dente, cook for less time; or if you prefer them softer, cook for longer.

Once the soup is cooked, add the noodles to the soup and serve right away.

FOR LITTLE HANDS: Allow your little one to help spiral cut the squash while supervised. Placing the veggies into the pressure cooker, slow cooker or stock pot is also a great job for them.

Meat Pockets

GRAIN FREE, GLUTEN FREE, DAIRY FREE, NUT FREE, EGG FREE, SOY FREE

Call it a pasty, a meat pocket, a hand pie or just plain delicious, this is a handy little bread filled with meat and veggies perfect for making ahead and popping into the lunch box. They're also great for picnics and dinners as they pack a great balance of nutrients into one handheld portable pocket.

MAKES: 8 SERVINGS

FOR THE DOUGH

1 cup (128 g) cassava flour

⅓ cup (80 ml) melted ghee

1 tsp sea salt

2 tbsp (30 ml) local honey

1 cup (240 ml) warm water

¼ cup (28 g) flax meal (I prefer the mild taste of brown flax vs. golden flax)

1 tbsp (9 g) psyllium husk powder

FOR THE FILLING

¼ cup (32 g) carrots, chopped

½ medium onion, chopped

¼ cup (32 g) zucchini, chopped

1 pound (455 g) grass-fed ground beef

1 tsp garlic sea salt

¼ tsp black pepper

½ tsp onion powder

1 tbsp (2 g) dried parsley

2 tsp (10 g) avocado oil, ghee, olive oil or preferred cooking fat

Preheat the oven to 350°F (175°C).

Make the dough, by combining the ingredients in a bowl and kneading until you have a ball of dough. Divide the dough into 8 equal sized pieces and set aside, covered.

Cook the veggies, beef and seasonings in a large skillet over medium/high heat in the cooking fat. Make sure meat is browned and no longer pink and the vegetables are slightly soft, around 10 minutes.

Roll or pat out one piece of dough until it is about ⅛-inch (3-mm) thick. Place a couple tablespoons of the meat mixture into the center of the disc of dough. Bring the edges of the dough together to envelope the meat and twist to secure. Flip the meat pocket over onto a parchment-lined baking sheet so the sealed side is against the parchment paper. Poke a couple of holes in the top of the dough and bake for 30 minutes. Remove and allow to cool slightly before serving.

 FOR LITTLE HANDS: Allow your child to help mix the dough ingredients, knead it and roll or pat it out. Your little helper can also help fill the dough with the meat mixture. Older children can help cook the meat and veggies in the skillet.

Ham + "Cheese" Quesadillas

GRAIN FREE, GLUTEN FREE, DAIRY FREE, EGG FREE, SOY FREE, NUT FREE

These make the perfect lunch box companion and assemble really easily. Just start with a batch of my Tortillas (page 61), which you can make ahead, and you'll have a quick meal in no time!

MAKES: 6 SERVINGS

6 Tortillas (page 61)

1 batch Nut-Free "Cheese" (page 53)

3 ounces (85 g) pasture raised ham, thinly sliced

1 tbsp (15 ml) avocado oil, ghee or preferred cooking fat

Make a batch of tortillas, but instead of grilling them on both sides, grill just one side (of each tortilla) to help it set. Then place an ounce (28 g) of "cheese" and an ounce (28 g) of ham between two tortillas, placing the cooked sides out and the uncooked sides against the fillings. Be careful handling them as they are more fragile before cooking them through.

Heat the cooking fat in a large skillet over high heat. Grill the quesadilla on both sides until the "cheese" is melted and the tortillas are cooked through, about 3 minutes per side. When flipping your quesadilla, use a thin flexible spatula to help keep the quesadilla from falling apart. Repeat with remaining ingredients until you have 3 quesadillas. You will likely have leftover "cheese" which you can slice and use on crackers or use in the Grilled "Cheese" (page 53) or Pizza Pocket (page 62) recipes.

 FOR LITTLE HANDS: Allow your child to help press out the tortillas with the tortilla press and help assemble the quesadillas. Older helpers may help grill them as well.

Use two halves cooked on one side only to make 1 quesadilla

Leave the uncooked halves open for the fillings

Stack fillings on one half, place other half on top (uncooked side facing filling)

Grill quesadilla on both sides until fillings melt and are heated through

Pizza Pockets

GRAIN FREE, GLUTEN FREE, DAIRY FREE, EGG FREE, SOY FREE, NUT FREE

Another fantastic lunch box filler, these pizza pockets are both dairy and grain free. Make these ahead and have school lunches for the week!

MAKES: 6 SERVINGS

6 Tortillas (page 61)

1 batch Nut-Free "Cheese" (page 53)

6 ounces (170 g) pasture-raised pepperoni

1 batch Easy Pizza Sauce (page 178), or organic store-bought

Preheat the oven to 350°F (175°C).

Make a batch of tortillas, but instead of grilling them, place an ounce (28 g) of "cheese" and an ounce (28 g) of pepperoni on half of a pressed tortilla. Place a small dollop of pizza sauce on top of the fillings and carefully fold the unfilled half of the tortilla over top the filled half. Use a fork to seal the edges all the way around so the fillings do not escape. Repeat with the remaining ingredients (you may have leftover "cheese") and then transfer them all to a parchment-lined baking sheet. Pierce the tops just slightly with a fork and then bake for approximately 20 minutes. Remove from the oven and serve after allowing them to cool slightly.

FOR LITTLE HANDS: Allow your child to help press the tortillas and to help fill them. They can be fragile so take care.

Mac 'N' "Cheese"

GRAIN FREE, GLUTEN FREE, DAIRY FREE, NUT FREE, SOY FREE

Oh yes, the famous mac 'n' cheese. If ever there was a food unanimously loved by the under-10 community, this would have to be it! I've created this recipe for gluten- and dairy-free kids everywhere in the hopes that they'll never feel deprived! Feel free to smother this "cheese" sauce on just about anything, I won't judge!

MAKES: 4 SERVINGS

FOR THE SAUCE

2 cups (480 ml) flax, coconut or almond milk

5 tbsp (20 g) nutritional yeast (or more if desired, this provides the cheesy flavor)

3 tbsp (45 g) avocado oil, olive oil or preferred fat

3 tsp (15 g) tomato sauce

¼ tsp garlic powder

¼ tsp onion powder

¼ tsp (or less) dry mustard

½ tsp apple cider vinegar (this provides a little tang)

Pinch paprika

¼ tsp (or less) turmeric

Salt to taste (I used about ½ tsp)

¼ cup (55 g) ghee (or less), optional for a "buttery" taste

Bay leaf

2-3 tbsp (16-24 g) tapioca flour

FOR THE NOODLES

1 cup (128 g) cassava flour (not tapioca starch)

2-3 pastured eggs

3-4 tbsp (45-60 g) cooking fat (olive oil, avocado oil, ghee)

½ tsp or more sea salt

To make the "cheese" sauce, combine all ingredients in a saucepan except for the tapioca (this includes ghee + bay leaf if using). The turmeric is mostly for color, but if you like turmeric you can go up to ¼ teaspoon. If you are sensitive to the flavor, start with just a pinch and go up from there. Bring to a simmer, whisking continually. Taste and add in more of the seasonings or dilute with more milk if necessary. Once the flavor has been adjusted, make a slurry with 1 tablespoon (8 g) of the tapioca by removing 3 tablespoons (45 ml) of the cheese sauce from the sauce pan and mixing in the tapioca. Reintroduce the slurry back into the cheese sauce, whisking until it begins to thicken. Repeat steps 4 and 5 until the desired thickness has been reached. Turn heat to low and make your pasta.

To make the noodles, bring 8 cups (1900 ml) of water to a boil on the stovetop over high heat (add a pinch of salt if desired). Combine all the noodle ingredients in a mixing bowl and use your hands to knead into a ball of dough. The dough should feel like dense glutenous dough once combined thoroughly. Lightly dust an area with a bit of cassava flour. Pinch off around one-sixth of the dough and roll it into a thin "snake," around ⅛-inch (3-mm) thick. Slice the snake into 1-inch (2.5-cm) pieces and pinch them to make them C shaped. Repeat with remaining dough. See photos in the Homemade Grain-Free Pasta (page 163) for a photo tutorial. Transfer the to the boiling water and let them cook until they float, just a few minutes. Using a slotted spoon, remove them from the water and transfer them to a strainer.

Ladle the "cheese" sauce over the cooked noodles and serve warm.

 FOR LITTLE HANDS: Allow your child to combine the ingredients and knead the dough. Your helper may also enjoy rolling the dough out with a rolling pin. Your child may also whisk the sauce ingredients while supervised.

Grain-Free Corn Dog Dippers

GRAIN FREE, GLUTEN FREE, DAIRY FREE, EGG FREE, NUT FREE, SOY FREE

I don't know about you, but going to the county fair (and my local shopping mall) brings back memories of growing up with fresh-squeezed lemonade and corn dogs!!! Crispy fried breading with a juicy, savory hot dog dipped into ketchup and honey mustard just can't be beat. Feed your kids the best of both worlds by combining organic grass-fed hot dogs with grain-free goodness sweetened only with local honey. Everybody wins!

MAKES: 4 SERVINGS

2 cups (480 g) oil for frying (avocado oil, coconut oil or sustainable palm shortening preferred)

4 grass-fed hot dogs

16 cookie sticks/lollipop sticks

⅓ cup (42 g) tapioca starch

2 tbsp (20 g) potato starch

2 tbsp (12 g) coconut flour

3 tbsp (21 g) sweet potato flour

1 cup (240 ml) dairy-free milk (flax, coconut, almond)

¼ cup (60 ml) local honey

½ tsp baking soda

Pinch sea salt

Honey Mustard (page 170)

Ketchup (page 174)

Heat the frying oil to approximately 325°F (163°C) in a small, deep saucepan. Using a larger saucepan will cause the oil to be more shallow and therefore will cover less surface area on your corn dog dippers.

Slice each hot dog into 4 bite-sized pieces. Stick a lollipop stick into the center of each hot dog bite; you will have 16 pieces total.

Mix the tapioca, potato starch, coconut flour, sweet potato flour, dairy-free milk, honey, baking soda and sea salt together in a mixing bowl and stir to combine. Because flour brands vary in their absorption, you may need a little more or less liquid to reach the desired consistency. Add a tablespoon (10 g) at a time if you need more until you have a thick cake-like batter.

Take one skewered hot dog and dip it into the batter, making sure to coat it completely but without excess. Quickly transfer it to the hot oil, holding it by the stick and swirl it left and right while frying it. Because there is no egg, the batter will want to fry off of the hot dog, but spinning it will help keep it adhered until it starts to harden. Once the batter appears more stable, around 30 seconds, you may lay the skewered dog on its side and allow it to fry until golden brown and crisped. Remove it from the hot oil and set it on a towel-lined plate, with the stick upright. Repeat with the remaining hot dog bites. Serve with my Honey Mustard and Ketchup.

 FOR LITTLE HANDS: Your child can help by slicing the hot dogs (with a child friendly knife), mixing the batter and skewering the hot dog bites. The frying is likely best left to grown up hands as the oil is very hot.

Teriyaki Meatballs + Daikon Noodles

GRAIN FREE, GLUTEN FREE, DAIRY FREE, EGG FREE, SOY FREE

These easy-peasy meatballs are great for weeknight dinners when you've got a busy schedule of soccer, piano, gymnastics and underwater basket weaving. Our favorite part of these is the sweet accent from the pure maple syrup balanced with the savory garlic flavors from the coconut aminos and seasonings. Talented kids still deserve a nutritious meal, so serve these over some quick daikon noodles and call it a night!

MAKES: 4 SERVINGS

1 pound (455 g) ground turkey meat

2 tbsp (30 ml) full-fat coconut milk

3 tbsp (22 g) tapioca starch

2 tbsp (30 ml) coconut aminos

1 tbsp (15 ml) 100% maple syrup

½ tsp minced garlic

¼ tsp ground ginger

Pinch salt

2 tbsp (30 ml) avocado oil (or coconut oil melted), divided

Freshly minced chives

2 large daikon radishes, spiral cut or julienned

Preheat the oven to 350°F (175°C).

Combine all ingredients except radishes and 1 tablespoon (15 ml) of oil in a mixing bowl and blend well with hands. Make meatballs about 2 inches (5 cm) in diameter and place onto a parchment-lined baking sheet. Bake for 25 minutes.

I also love making extra sauce from the ingredients above (omitting the meat and tapioca) and serving with daikon spiral cut noodles. To make the noodles, heat the remaining tablespoon (15 ml) of cooking fat in a large skillet over high heat. Add in the spiral-cut daikon and cook over high heat for around 8 to 10 minutes or until the extra moisture cooks off and the noodles are soft and heated through. If you want them browned, you can increase the sauté time until they reach your desired texture and doneness. Ladle the extra sauce over the noodles and serve right away with the meatballs.

 FOR LITTLE HANDS: Allow your child to help mix and shape the meatballs. Your helper can help spiral cut the daikon noodles as well.

Healing Foods

When your little one is feeling yucky, the last thing you want to offer is corn-syrup-based soda or gluten-based crackers! And while the Bananas, Rice, Applesauce and Toast (BRAT) diet is tried and true, if you are enforcing a grain-free household, removing the R + T leaves a BA diet behind!

So I've written some recipes to help get some nutrients into your little one and also aid in their healing. Creamy Papaya"sick"les with Electrolytes (page 83), Dairy-Free Coconut Yogurt (page 80) and Bone Broth (page 72) will help ensure your sick kid returns to your super kid before long!

Bone Broth

GRAIN FREE, GLUTEN FREE, DAIRY FREE, NUT FREE, EGG FREE, SOY FREE

There's a good reason that chicken soup is known for its magical healing effects...because it really does! There are anti-inflammatory effects of bone broth as well as gut-healing gelatin. Keep this broth on hand by freezing some for when little ones are feeling yucky!

MAKES: 10 SERVINGS (DEPENDING ON SLOW COOKER SIZE)

1–2 pounds (455–910 g) chicken or beef bones

2 tbsp (30 ml) apple cider vinegar (to pull minerals from bones)

4 large carrots

2 onions, chopped in half with skins on

One small bunch soup greens (leek, dill, parsley, etc)

3–4 stalks celery

Bay leaf

1 tsp garlic powder or 3 cloves fresh

Ground black pepper

Water

If you are using chicken bones, you can place all ingredients into the slow cooker and fill to the top with water.

If making beef broth, preheat oven to 350°F (175°C) and place beef bones on a baking sheet. Bake the bones for 30 minutes. Place in a slow cooker with the remaining ingredients and fill to the top with water.

Turn the slow cooker onto the lowest setting and allow the soup to cook for up to 3 days. If your slow cooker has an automatic turn off switch, be sure to navigate by this so that it does not stop cooking while you are sleeping or away from your home. My preference is 36 to 48 hour bone broth. You can also reuse the bones to make additional batches of soup. Use them until they are brittle.

Strain the broth from the veggies, herbs and bones and freeze in smaller amounts if you batch cook. Otherwise use it for soups, stews, gravies and so on. Do not over-salt your broth as you will likely salt it later as you reheat it for different purposes. You can always add salt later as you develop it into other recipes.

Notes: The onion skins will help yield a dark, rich colored broth. If you desire extra gelatin you can include chicken feet in your broth.

 FOR LITTLE HANDS: Allow your child to place all the ingredients into the slow cooker (except for hot bones if making beef broth).

Banana Pudding

GRAIN FREE, GLUTEN FREE, DAIRY FREE, EGG FREE, NUT FREE, SOY FREE

Remember that good ol' classic banana pudding with vanilla wafers and loads of sugar?! Eeks! I've made a version here that is not only delicious, it's the perfect soothing food when not much else sounds appealing.

MAKES: 2 SERVINGS

2 bananas, sliced

1 (13½ ounce [370 ml]) can full-fat (or reduced fat) coconut milk

1½ tsp (7 ml) pure vanilla extract

2 tbsp (15 g) tapioca starch

2–3 tbsp (30–45 ml) pure maple syrup

Optional: Vanilla Wafers (page 95)

Whisk all the ingredients together in a saucepan. Turn the heat on medium and continue whisking until the pudding mixture starts to thicken, and all ingredients are well combined. Once the desired consistency is met, remove the pudding from heat and pour into individual bowls. Top with sliced bananas and Vanilla Wafers if serving as a dessert rather than as a tummy soother.

 FOR LITTLE HANDS: With supervision, allow your child to help whisk the pudding mixture or slice the bananas with a child safe knife.

Cinnamon Applesauce

GRAIN FREE, GLUTEN FREE, DAIRY FREE, EGG FREE, NUT FREE, SOY FREE

The traditional BRAT diet includes applesauce, which can often be laden with excess sugar. That sugar is capable of upsetting that tummy even more! Why not make an easy homemade version with cinnamon to help digestion and collagen to help soothe tummies?

MAKES: 5 SERVINGS

5 apples, any variety
½ cup (120 ml) 100% apple juice or cider
1 tbsp (8 g) ground cinnamon
3 tbsp (21 g) grass-fed collagen powder

Core and seed apples and coarsely chop.

If using a pressure cooker or Instant Pot, place apples, ground cinnamon and juice into cooker. Secure the lid and manually select 5 minutes on high pressure. Once complete, quick release the pressure and when appropriate, remove the lid.

If using a slow cooker, place chopped apples, cinnamon and juice into the slow cooker and cook on low for 4 hours.

When cooked, transfer contents to a blender or use an immersion blender to purée into sauce. Once smooth, add in the grass-fed collagen and stir to combine. Chill and serve.

 FOR LITTLE HANDS: Using a child safe knife (for younger helpers), allow your child to help chop the apples. Older kids may help operate the pressure cooker or slow cooker while supervised.

Ginger Chews

GRAIN FREE, GLUTEN FREE, DAIRY FREE, NUT FREE, EGG FREE, SOY FREE

Ginger is a long time naturally sourced aid for settling upset tummies. While raw ginger may be a bit strong for younger taste buds, these homemade ginger chews are naturally sweetened and much more palatable!

MAKES: 20 SERVINGS

1 cup (96 g) peeled, thinly sliced fresh ginger root

1 cup (240 ml) local honey

1 cup (240 ml) water

½ cup (96 g) maple sugar or coconut palm sugar

Combine the first 3 ingredients in a small saucepan. Turn the heat on medium high and bring the mixture to a boil. Stir to make sure the honey and water are fully combined. Allow the ginger to simmer for about 30 minutes.

Pour the maple sugar into a bowl and set aside. Remove the cooked ginger from the saucepan using a slotted spoon, leaving the excess thickened honey syrup behind. Roll the ginger slices in the maple sugar to coat them, shaking off the excess. Store the ginger chews in the fridge in an airtight container and use as needed.

 FOR LITTLE HANDS: Allow your child to dredge the ginger slices in the maple sugar. If older, your child may help peel or slice the ginger root while supervised.

Dairy-Free Coconut Yogurt

GRAIN FREE, GLUTEN FREE, DAIRY FREE, NUT FREE, EGG FREE, SOY FREE

Yogurt is great for tummies because of the probiotic content, but dairy-based yogurt can often be counterproductive as it can increase mucous production and upset an already upset stomach. My dairy-free yogurt is coconut milk based, so it is full of good fats yet easier to digest than dairy for those with sensitivities. Top this one with fruit or my Grain- + Nut-Free Granola (page 22).

MAKES: 3 SERVINGS

2 (13½ ounce [370 ml]) cans full-fat coconut milk

3 small heat resistant glass bowls or yogurt cups

1 tsp 100% vanilla extract

3 tbsp (45 ml) 100% maple syrup

2 tbsp (16 g) tapioca or arrowroot

1 tsp probiotic powder (I used 200 billion cfu)

Chill one can of coconut milk in the fridge for at least an hour. Sterilize the glass bowls with boiling water or by running them through the dishwasher. Set them aside.

In a medium saucepan, combine one can of coconut milk, the coconut cream from the top of the chilled can of coconut milk, vanilla and maple syrup over low heat. Stir or whisk until the cream is melted down and incorporated into the mix. Remove ¼ cup (22 g) of the mixture from the pot and whisk in the 2 tablespoons (16 g) starch. Reincorporate this slurry into the heated yogurt mixture. Stir once more, then remove the saucepan from heat.

Once the yogurt mixture has cooled to around 100°F (38°C), stir in the probiotic powder. Doing so prematurely may result in killing the bacteria, preventing its ability to culture properly so be sure to let the yogurt cool.

At this time if using a yogurt maker, you may fill the bowls with the yogurt mixture and then follow the directions of your yogurt machine. Once complete, transfer the bowls to the fridge (covered) to chill.

If you are using an Instant Pot, pour 1 cup (240 ml) of water into the stainless bowl of your Instant Pot. Fill your glass bowls with the yogurt mix and place them inside the Instant Pot bowl. If your bowls do not all fit at once, you may stack them on top of each other as long as they do not spill over. Secure the lid and select the Yogurt feature. Cook for 6 hours and then remove the lid, take out the yogurt bowls, cover them and transfer them to the refrigerator to firm up further.

If you are using a conventional oven, turn on the oven light, cover the saucepan with a lid and transfer it to the oven for at least 4 hours or until the yogurt is set. It will thicken best a little over 100°F (38°C) (and then will thicken further in the fridge). Remove the saucepan from the oven after the yogurt is set and serve right away or store in an airtight container in the refrigerator.

 FOR LITTLE HANDS: Allow your child to help whisk the ingredients, stir on the stovetop or pour into the glass bowls.

Papaya "sick" les with Electrolytes

GRAIN FREE, GLUTEN FREE, DAIRY FREE, NUT FREE, EGG FREE, SOY FREE

When kiddos feel yucky, it's hard to know what to feed them without aggravating already sensitive systems. These healthy, healing popsicles are the perfect solution when solids aren't quite back in the picture yet. The addition of collagen is extra gut healing too. Papaya helps sooth tummies and aid in digestion with special enzymes.

MAKES: 5 SERVINGS

2 cups (290 g) fresh diced papaya

⅔ cup (60 ml) full-fat coconut milk or unsweetened coconut water

Optional: ¼ cup (28 g) grass-fed collagen powder

Combine all of the ingredients in a blender and blend on high to puree until the mixture is smooth. Spoon the papaya mixture into the freezer molds and insert sticks. Freeze for 4 to 6 hours or until frozen through. To remove from the molds, run warm water on the outsides of the molds to help loosen them.

 FOR LITTLE HANDS: Allow your child to help blend the ingredients while supervised. Your helper can also help spoon the mixture into the molds.

Flu Season Gummies

GRAIN FREE, GLUTEN FREE, DAIRY FREE, NUT FREE, EGG FREE, SOY FREE

While the flu doesn't actually have a season, it tends to peak in winter months when stress is higher, diets are less clean and Vitamin D deficiencies surge with the absence of the sunny days of summer. These Flu Season Gummies sneak in some good stuff to help keep immune systems strong and able to fight off the yucks! Elderberry syrup is known to help reduce flu symptoms and severity and to provide immune support. It also may have anti-viral/anti-bacterial properties. Omit if you have a known sensitivity. Vitamin C helps keep immune systems operating at top notch by increasing white blood cells, and vitamin D is important for overall immune health and disease prevention. Local raw honey is immune supportive and may have anti-bacterial and anti-viral properties. Cranberries have been shown to reduce the severity and longevity of flu symptoms, it boosts NK (natural killer) cells, and has been shown to be immune supportive.

MAKES: 10 OR MORE SERVINGS

1 cup (240 ml) organic cranberry juice blend 100% juice, no sugar added

1 tbsp (15 ml) pure elderberry syrup, no sugar added

¼ cup (28 g) grass-fed gelatin (the kind that congeals)

3 drops vitamin D3 (3,000 IU total)

1 tsp vitamin C crystals (4,000 mg Vitamin C)

1 tbsp (15 ml) local raw honey

Optional: Echinacea drops (Not advised for use if you have an autoimmune disorder)

Combine juice and elderberry syrup in a small saucepan. Turn heat on medium/high and add in gelatin. Stir well to combine, leaving no gelatin lumps behind; this should take a minute or two. You'll want to heat it thoroughly but it is not necessary to boil as long as the gelatin is combined well. Add in the vitamin D drops and vitamin C powder. Remove from heat at once and stir in your honey. Pour the mixture into molds and refrigerate or freeze until set; this usually takes about half an hour or less if frozen.

One gummy has 67 IU vitamin D and 89 mg vitamin C.

FOR LITTLE HANDS: Have your wee one help stir the ingredients together in the saucepan or help pour the mixture (supervised as it's hot) into the molds. After they've set, your helper can pop them out of the molds too.

Snack Attack

If your kids are like mine, snack time can hit at any time of the day...right after breakfast, right before bed and most certainly at the most inconvenient times like when your car breaks down in the middle of nowhere. I learned long ago that if I were to have a fighting chance, I better be prepared for snack time whenever it might hit!

In this snack chapter, I have compiled a bunch of kid favorites—some ready in minutes and some to make ahead and have in stock. If you ever feel like you are giving your kids too much sugar, not enough nutrients and too many processed snacks, this chapter will help you navigate snack time and feel good about it! My kids go crazy for the Ladybug Veggie Bites (page 88), Lala Truffles (page 92), Paleo Piggies (page 112) and "Cheese" Quackers (page 100). I admittedly snack on them all too!

Ladybug Veggie Bites

GRAIN FREE, GLUTEN FREE, DAIRY FREE, EGG FREE, NUT FREE, SOY FREE

Sometimes veggies are just plain boring! And sometimes little mouths have no interest in eating them. These adorable Ladybug Veggie Bites are made solely from veggies and a little dollop of dairy-free ranch dressing and might just make your kiddo hop on board the veggie train!

MAKES: 5 SERVINGS

1 batch Ranch Dressing (page 173)

1 medium cucumber, sliced into 25 round slices

25 grape tomatoes, quartered lengthwise

Fresh chives cut into 1-inch (2.5-cm) long pieces

25 small black olives, pitted

Optional: ¼ tsp activated charcoal

Begin by making the Ranch Dressing. You may use less dairy-free milk and more mayo in order to make it thicker.

Slice the cucumbers about ⅛-inch (3-mm) thick and quarter the tomatoes. Chop the chives into 2-inch (5-cm) pieces.

Place about a teaspoon or less of the ranch dressing on each cucumber slice and arrange 2 of the tomato quarters on the dressing like wings, as indicated by the photo. Place a black olive at the head of the tomato wings. Slide two of the chive pieces into the pitted olive for the antennae.

If you wish to make the ladybug spots, mix the activated charcoal with a few drops of water until you make a paste. Using a toothpick or fork prong, dot the activated charcoal mixture onto the tomatoes. This step can be omitted if you do not have activated charcoal.

 FOR LITTLE HANDS: Using a child safe knife, allow your child to help slice the cucumbers or help stir the ranch dressing. The other steps may require more advanced fine motor skills, so older children might be best suited for those.

Great Grape Gummies

GRAIN FREE, GLUTEN FREE, DAIRY FREE, NUT FREE, EGG FREE, SOY FREE

Homemade gummies are just as fun as can be and with all of the easy-to-order silicone molds out there, you can basically gummify anything these days! The best part is these are made with only the best ingredients, so you don't have to worry about all the garbage in the store bought ones!

MAKES: 3 SERVINGS

1 cup (240 ml) organic grape juice
¼ cup (28 g) grass-fed gelatin
1 tsp 100% maple syrup
2 tsp (10 ml) apple cider vinegar (or more)

Combine all ingredients in a small saucepan over medium heat, whisking until heated through, about 2 minutes. Quickly remove from heat and carefully pour into silicone candy molds. Refrigerate for an hour or until firmed and then remove from the molds. Store these in the refrigerator in an airtight container for up to a week.

Note: You can cut the setting time by freezing, but keep an eye on them or they can freeze solid!

 FOR LITTLE HANDS: Allow your child to help whisk the ingredients while supervised. Older helpers may assist in pouring the hot mixture into the molds as well.

Lala Truffles

GRAIN FREE, GLUTEN FREE, DAIRY FREE, NUT FREE, EGG FREE, SOY FREE

If your kiddo is a snack bar lover, these are the perfect fit! With only four ingredients, you'll find they're easy to throw together to take on a road trip or even to the park. They are naturally sweet with the use of dates and have that fantastic crunch from the sunflower seeds and coconut! Plus they have no nuts, so they're allergy friendly!

MAKES: 9 SERVINGS

1 cup (150 g) pitted dates
¼ cup (56 g) dairy- and soy-free chocolate chips
¾ cup (105 g) sunflower seeds
½ cup (45 g) unsweetened shredded coconut, divided

Combine all of the ingredients (using only ¼ cup [24 g] of the coconut at this time) in a blender or food processor. Start blending on low and increase speed until the ingredients become fully combined and uniform. In a separate bowl, place the remaining ¼ cup (24 g) of coconut. Take a golfball-sized amount of the mixture and roll it into a truffle. Roll it in the coconut and set it aside. If your truffle is too dry, you can dampen it with a little bit of cool water before rolling it in the coconut. Some dates tend to be stickier than others. Repeat with remaining truffle mixture and serve right away or store in the refrigerator for later.

 FOR LITTLE HANDS: Allow your child to help shape the truffles and help roll them in the coconut. Older children may help operate the blender under supervision and complete this entire recipe start to finish!

Vanilla Wafers

GRAIN FREE, GLUTEN FREE, DAIRY FREE, NUT FREE, EGG FREE, SOY FREE

Remember hoarding a box of these wafers all to yourself and realizing that you could absolutely finish the entire thing? Well maybe that was just me, but these kid-faves are certainly addicting! I've recreated those vanilla cookies with my own crisped, honey-sweetened treat baked with brown butter ghee for an inventive twist that will satisfy that same traditional craving!

MAKES: 5 SERVINGS

1 cup (128 g) high-quality cassava flour

1 tsp baking soda

¼ tsp sea salt

½ cup (120 g) brown butter ghee, plain ghee or coconut oil (ghee preferred)

5 tbsp (75 ml) local honey

1½ tsp (7 ml) pure vanilla extract

1 tbsp (7 g) grass-fed gelatin (the variety that congeals)

Preheat the oven to 350°F (175°C).

Combine all ingredients in a bowl and stir well. Take a heaping teaspoon of dough and roll it between your palms. On a parchment-lined baking sheet press the ball of dough into a disc. Repeat with the remaining dough. You can leave only a little space between cookies as they will not spread while baking.

Bake them for about 10 minutes, the edges may start to slightly brown. Remove the baking sheet and allow the cookies to cool. They have a slight shortbread consistency after cooling and are buttery and delicious!

These should stay crisped at room temperature storage. If not, give them a quick toast in your toaster oven on a low setting to crisp them back up!

 FOR LITTLE HANDS: Allow your child to stir the ingredients in the mixing bowl, or pre-measure the ingredients and they can combine them in the bowl.

Orange Dreamysicle Gummies

GRAIN FREE, GLUTEN FREE, DAIRY FREE, NUT FREE, EGG FREE, SOY FREE

Homemade gummies are a fun, healthy treat that parents can feel so much more confident about feeding to their kiddos! These are reminiscent of an orange push pop—creamy orange yummies molded right into gummies! Always a childhood favorite, these are free of refined sugar, packed with gut-healing gelatin and really fun to eat!

MAKES: 3 SERVINGS

1 cup (240 ml) organic orange juice

¼ cup (28 g) gelatin (the variety that can congeal)

1 tsp local honey

¼ cup (60 ml) coconut cream

10 drops orange stevia OR 2 tsp (10 ml) honey

Lemon juice to taste

Stir all ingredients in a small saucepan over medium heat until warmed through and well combined, around 4 minutes or less. Quickly remove from heat and carefully pour into molds with kid-friendly shapes like robots, dinosaurs, hearts, flowers or favorite characters. Refrigerate for 30 minutes or until firmed and then gently pop the gummies out of the molds. Store in an airtight container or zip top bag in the refrigerator until ready to use.

FOR LITTLE HANDS: Allow your supervised child to stir the ingredients in the saucepan. Pouring the hot liquid into the molds can be a bit more complicated and is often times better when left to an adult or older child.

Graham Crackers

GRAIN FREE, GLUTEN FREE, DAIRY FREE, EGG FREE, NUT FREE, SOY FREE

Always a favorite, these grain-free grahams are also egg- and nut-free! Snack on them plain or make some S'mores (page 206) for an extra special treat!

MAKES: 10 SERVINGS

1 tbsp (7 g) ground flax seed

1 tsp baking soda

¾ cup (72 g) coconut flour

¼ cup (30 g) tapioca starch

½ tbsp (7 g) molasses

3 tbsp (45 g) coconut oil, ghee or avocado oil

1 tsp 100% vanilla extract

¼ cup (60 ml) 100% maple syrup

Preheat the oven to 350°F (175°C).

Combine all ingredients in a mixing bowl. If you have flax meal, you can use that, otherwise simply mill your own flax seeds until a fine powder forms. Once ingredients are mixed well, roll the dough out between two pieces of parchment paper until it is about ⅛-inch (3-mm) thick. If your dough seems too dry and crumbly, add a bit more fat or maple syrup. If it seems too wet to roll, add a bit more coconut flour. Different brands of coconut flours can behave differently so adjust accordingly.

Once the dough is rolled out, remove the top sheet of paper and score the dough with desired cracker shapes and sizes with a pizza cutter or paring knife. Poke holes into each cracker to minimize puffing as the crackers bake. Bake for 8 to 10 minutes and remove them to cool before breaking them apart. If your crackers are a little thicker, you'll need to bake them a few minutes extra to get them to crisp up.

FOR LITTLE HANDS: Allow your child to help combine ingredients and mix them in the bowl. They can also help poke holes or use the pizza cutter to slice the dough!

"Cheese" Quackers

GRAIN FREE, GLUTEN FREE, DAIRY FREE, EGG FREE, NUT FREE, SOY FREE

You won't believe these crackers are allergy-friendly and free of cheese! My special blend of ingredients will fool even the most discerning eyes and taste buds! Store these in an airtight container and toast them to crisp them back up in the event that they lose their perfect texture in storage!

MAKES: 5 SERVINGS

1 cup (128 g) cassava flour

¼ cup (60 g) ghee

¼ cup (60 ml) olive oil

½ cup (120 ml) coconut milk or other dairy-free milk

½ tsp turmeric

Up to 1 tsp sea salt

2 tbsp (30 ml) Ketchup (page 174) or high-quality store-bought

3–4 tbsp (10–15 g) nutritional yeast

½ tsp or more onion powder

¼ tsp garlic powder

Preheat the oven to 350°F (175°C).

Combine all the ingredients in a mixing bowl. You can begin mixing them with a spoon, but kneading by hand will ensure that all ingredients are incorporated well and the color is a solid cheesy orange. Once the dough is uniform, roll it out between two pieces of parchment paper until it is about ⅛-inch (3-mm) thick. Remove the top sheet of parchment paper and slice them into square crackers, or cut into shapes using a mini cookie cutter.

Poke a hole in each cracker and bake them for around 10 minutes (or more). Because ovens vary, you may need to bake them longer in order to get them crisp, sometimes closer to 18 minutes. The thickness of your quackers will also determine how long they should be baked. They will crisp up more after cooling as well. Remove after baking, allow them to cool and then serve. Store them in an airtight container for up to a week, unrefrigerated.

To crisp the quackers up again before serving, simply pop them into the toaster oven on a baking sheet and run one short cycle to prevent burning.

 FOR LITTLE HANDS: Let your child help combine all the ingredients in the mixing bowl. You can also allow your child to help with the cookie cutter stamping or using the pizza cutter to slice, supervised of course!

Gummy Worms

GRAIN FREE, GLUTEN FREE, DAIRY FREE, EGG FREE, NUT FREE, SOY FREE

Why these squiggly invertebrates ever became a desired treat is beyond me, but we all know kids are fans in the biggest way! And if you've ever read the label on these squirmies, it likely made you squirm too! I have made them here with only fruit-sweetened juice and grass-fed gelatin, so you can let the wriggly feast begin and not have a worry in the world (except maybe finding one of these strategically placed to freak you out)!

MAKES: 2-3 SERVINGS

2 cups (480 ml) tart 100% fruit juice (this will also be the color of your worms)

3 tbsp (21 g) grass-fed gelatin (must be able to congeal versus collagen, which does not)

Start by combining the fruit juice and gelatin in a small saucepan over low/medium heat, stirring well to combine. This usually takes only a minute or so until the gelatin is dissolved completely. Remove the warm mixture from the stove top.

Group 20 to 30 wide-mouth straws in a bunch, securing them with the rubber bands until they cannot move. In a large glass or jar, pour about 2 to 3 tablespoons (30 to 45 ml) of the juice mixture into the bottom. Now place the banded straws into the mason jar so the juice mixture can fill the very bottoms of the inserted straws. Make sure the straws are vertical or the "plugs" will not form in the bottom of the straws—this is a necessary step before moving forward. Now refrigerate the straws and mason jar until the bottom gelatin is set, anywhere from 10 to 20 minutes. Place the remaining juice back onto a warm burner so it does not set in the saucepan.

Pour the remaining juice mixture into the straws, distributing evenly. You will want to leave a little space at the top of each straw to allow for easier removal. Refrigerate once more for about 30 minutes (sometimes longer). Pull the straws out of the rubber bands and briefly run them under warm water. Pinch the straw from the end with the space and begin squeezing the "worms" out the other end. To store, place them in an airtight container like a resealable bag so that they are not exposed to air (or they will dry out). The worms can last up to a week refrigerated.

 FOR LITTLE HANDS: While supervised, your child can help whisk the gelatin into the juice and pour the mixture into the straws.

Animal Crackers

GRAIN FREE, GLUTEN FREE, DAIRY FREE, NUT FREE, EGG FREE, SOY FREE

Generation after generation, animal crackers have been a childhood favorite. Who hasn't bitten the head off a lion or made their camel run? I believe no child should have to experience the world without an animal cracker, especially those suffering from food sensitivities! These are completely allergy-friendly and are just as much fun as the originals!

MAKES: 6 SERVINGS

⅓ cup (40 g) tapioca starch

⅓ cup (54 g) potato starch

6 tbsp (36 g) coconut flour

¼ cup (60 ml) melted sustainable palm shortening

⅓ cup (80 ml) local honey

1 tsp baking soda

Pinch sea salt

Preheat the oven to 300°F (150°C).

Combine all of the ingredients in a mixing bowl, stirring first and then kneading by hand until you've formed a ball of cookie dough.

Roll the dough out between two pieces of parchment paper until it is about ⅛-inch (3-mm) thick. Remove the top sheet of parchment and use cookie cutters to punch out a variety of shapes. Leave them in place as they are fragile if transferred unbaked. Remove the excess dough between the animal shapes and roll it out between two additional pieces of parchment paper, repeating the above steps.

Bake for between 10 to 15 minutes and then remove from the oven to cool. If your animal crackers are not as crisp as you'd like, you may return them to the oven for a few more minutes or toast them in your toaster oven until desired texture is achieved.

Store them in an airtight container for up to a week, toasting them for a quick cycle in your toaster oven if they need to be crisped up.

 FOR LITTLE HANDS: Let your child combine the dough ingredients or help punch animal shapes with the cookie cutters!

Soft Pretzels

GRAIN FREE, GLUTEN FREE, DAIRY FREE, NUT FREE, SOY FREE

You know that smell when you walk by a pretzel store in a shopping mall? Or by a bakery that bakes soft pretzels? It's like they figured out the secret of the universe and bottled its heavenly aroma. Well, I think we all deserve that goodness, so I've made my version of a soft pretzel that's free of grain, gluten and dairy and made it nut-free to boot! I recommend coarse salt and melted ghee to make this recipe even more delightful!

MAKES: 4 LARGE SERVINGS OR 8 SMALL

FOR THE WATER BATH

10 cups (2.5 L) water

1 tbsp (15 ml) apple cider vinegar

1 tbsp (18 g) sea salt

FOR THE PRETZELS

1 cup (240 ml) warm water (around 110°F [43°C])

1 packet gluten-free quick acting yeast

1 tbsp (15 ml) 100% maple syrup

1 pastured egg

½ cup (64 g) potato starch

½ cup (64 g) cassava flour

2 tbsp (18 g) psyllium husk powder

1 tbsp (12 g) coconut flour

4 tbsp (60 g) ghee, avocado oil, olive oil or preferred cooking fat, divided

1 tsp baking soda

¼ tsp sea salt

2 tbsp (30 g) coarse sea salt

Preheat oven to 425°F (218°C). Bring the water bath ingredients to a boil in a large pot.

Combine the cup (240 ml) of warm water, yeast and maple syrup in a mixing bowl. Allow the yeast to multiply, for about 5 to 10 minutes. If it doesn't froth or foam, toss the mixture and begin again. Either the yeast was dead or it was killed by the temperature of the water.

Once your yeast mixture is frothy, add in the remaining pretzel ingredients, except the coarse salt and 2 tablespoons (30 g) of the cooking fat, and stir to combine. It now becomes easier to use your hands to combine the ingredients together more thoroughly. If making 4 large pretzels, divide the dough into 4 large pieces. If making smaller pretzels, divide the dough into 8 equal sized pieces.

Roll one of the dough pieces into a long snake about 18-inches (45-cm) long (shorter for the small pretzels) and then make a U shape. Twist the two ends of the "U" together, crossing once then twisting again and bring them to the base of the U where you can secure the twist by pressing it into the base. Transfer the pretzel to the boiling water bath and allow it to cook for about 3 minutes. Remove the pretzel with a skimmer and transfer it to a parchment-lined baking sheet. Repeat with the remaining dough. You can just make straight pretzel twists without having them be a traditional pretzel shape.

Once all of the dough pieces have been boiled, baste them with the remaining 2 tablespoons (30 g) of ghee or cooking fat, sprinkle with the coarse sea salt bake them for 15 to 20 minutes. The longer you bake them, the crispier the exterior will become. The inside should be soft. These are best the same day or frozen and reheated in the toaster oven or conventional oven.

FOR LITTLE HANDS: Allow your child to help mix the pretzel ingredients and to help shape the dough. If pretzel shapes are difficult, allow your child to help roll out the snakes.

Monkey Toes (Filled Dates)

GRAIN FREE, GLUTEN FREE, DAIRY FREE, NUT FREE, EGG FREE, SOY FREE

Finding allergy-friendly snacks that are easy to toss together yet more exciting than carrot sticks can be a challenge. These Monkey Toes are easy enough for the little ones to assemble, and they'll have just as much fun devouring them! Made with sweet sunflower butter and dates, they take a chewy sweet vehicle to deliver the creamy peanut butter-like filling, sprinkled with cinnamon. This snack is filled with B vitamins, potassium, fiber and essential fatty acids all while tasting like a dessert! These are one of my son's favorite snacks, and he even makes them for friends who come visit!

MAKES: 4 SERVINGS

¼ cup (60 g) Sunflower Seed Butter (page 111)

12 pitted Medjool dates

Ground cinnamon to taste

Spoon the sunflower seed butter into a piping bag or resealable bag with a corner cut. Fill one of the dates by piping the sunflower seed butter into the area where the pit was removed. Sprinkle with ground cinnamon to taste and repeat until all the dates are filled.

 FOR LITTLE HANDS: This is a great recipe to encourage autonomy in the kitchen. Your littles, depending on age, may be able to assemble these entirely on their own. If you are pitting your own dates, this might be an area where adult assistance is needed.

Paleo Piggies

GRAIN FREE, GLUTEN FREE, DAIRY FREE, NUT FREE, EGG FREE, SOY FREE

One of my favorite party food appetizers, I've served these at everything from my kids' birthday parties to adult gatherings, and they are always the first to go! These certainly don't use dough from a can, but they are always a hit nonetheless!

MAKES: 6 SERVINGS

1 cup (128 g) cassava flour

⅓ cup (80 ml) melted ghee or preferred cooking fat

1 tsp sea salt

2 tbsp (30 ml) local honey

1 cup (240 ml) warm water

¼ cup (28 g) flax meal (I prefer the mild taste of brown flax)

1 tbsp (9 g) psyllium husk powder

12 oz (340 g) grass-fed mini hot dogs

Honey Mustard (page 170), optional

Preheat the oven to 350°F (175°C).

Combine all of the ingredients, except for the hot dogs and Honey Mustard and knead together until you can form a ball of dough. Divide the dough into 4 equal pieces. Take one piece and roll it out in to a round flat disk about ⅛-inch (3-mm) thick. Slice it like a pie into 8 triangles. Roll one hot dog into one triangles, starting at the widest part of the triangle and rolling towards the point. Place that dough wrapped dog on a parchment-lined baking sheet. Repeat with the remaining dough and dogs. Bake the piggies for 15 minutes and remove from the oven. Allow them to cool slightly and serve alone or with Honey Mustard for dipping.

FOR LITTLE HANDS: Allow your child to help mix the dough and knead it. Your little helper can also help roll the dough out and roll the hot dogs into the triangles. Do not worry if they aren't perfect; they'll be delicious nonetheless!

Sidekicks

Veggies got you stumped? Kids aren't into kale and cauli? I hear your cries for help, and I totally understand. Sometimes veggies are like the forbidden zone when it comes to getting your kiddo to try new foods. What can possibly be done?

Well, a few things, starting with the recipes in this chapter. I have personally run all these side dishes by my three test pilots, and only the approved recipes made the book. They are savory, healthy and kid-approved, so you can rest assured there will be no throwing vegetables across the table! The Give Peas a Chance Fritters (page 125), Parsnip Fries (page 121) and BFF Brussels (page 129) are so good my kids have been known to fight over them.

Sweet Potato Bacon Tots

GRAIN FREE, GLUTEN FREE, DAIRY FREE, NUT FREE, EGG FREE, SOY FREE

Most tater tots are made with pretty unsavory ingredients, and for those who are extra sensitive to cross contamination, eating them out becomes basically impossible. I made these with sweet potato and bacon for a flavor kick and no risk of the yucky stuff like rancid oils or traces of gluten!

MAKES: 4 SERVINGS

1 large sweet potato

5 strips of crispy bacon, chopped

Up to 1 tsp garlic sea salt (to taste)

½ tsp onion powder

½ tsp ground black pepper

½ cup (80 g) potato starch or cassava flour

Avocado oil or light olive oil for frying

Awesome Sauce (page 177), optional

Boil the sweet potato submerged in water for about 10 minutes. Remove the sweet potato from the boiling water and once cool enough to handle, peel or slice the skin off. Grate the sweet potato, using a hand grater, mandolin or food processor.

Once the sweet potato is grated, use a hand towel or a few paper towels to squeeze out the excess water from the potato. This step is important, as you do not want to have soggy tots!

Add the other ingredients (minus the oil and sauce) to the grated sweet potato in a mixing bowl and combine by hand. Preheat oil for frying in a large skillet over medium/high heat; it does not need to be enough oil for deep frying, but it should be enough to generously cover the bottom of the skillet.

While the cooking oil heats, begin shaping your tots. Roll about a tablespoon (15 g) of the dough into a ball, and then elongate it and flatten the ends to give it that distinctive tot shape.

Fry the tots, rolling them around on all sides to make sure they crisp up. Once all sides are cooked, around 5 minutes or more, use a slotted spoon or skimmer to remove the tots and transfer them to a towel-lined plate to cool slightly. Serve alone or with my Awesome Sauce.

 FOR LITTLE HANDS: Allow your child to help shape the tots. It's okay if they are not shaped perfectly as they will fry deliciously regardless. Older kids can help fry the tots while supervised.

Parsnip Fries

GRAIN FREE, GLUTEN FREE, DAIRY FREE, EGG FREE, NUT FREE, SOY FREE

Need more ways to sneak in veggies? These parsnip fries are so dynamite, your little ones won't miss potatoes for a second. They also make a great lower starch alternative!

MAKES: 4 SERVINGS

3 medium parsnips

Avocado oil, coconut oil or ghee for frying

Sea salt to taste

Optional: garlic powder

Peel the parsnips like a carrot.

Preheat the frying fat over medium/high heat, on the higher side for about 5 minutes while you cut the parsnips.

Slice the parsnips into fries, on the thinner side if you prefer crispy or thicker if you like softer fries, like steak fries. Kids can be particular in their texture preferences so parsnips are very accommodating in this way.

Fry the sliced parsnips in the preheated oil until they are browned and crisped. If you've cut them very thin, be careful they do not burn, as the more shoestring they become, the faster they will cook and the more sensitive to heat they become.

Once they've reached desired doneness, use a skimmer or slotted spoon to remove them from the oil and transfer them to a towel lined plate. Season with sea salt and garlic powder if desired. Serve warm!

 FOR LITTLE HANDS: Allow your child to help cut the parsnips into fries with a kid-proof safe knife.

Mimi's Little Veggie Trees

GRAIN FREE, GLUTEN FREE, DAIRY FREE, EGG FREE, NUT FREE, SOY FREE

When my son was little, we had to come up with ways to get him to try new foods. Because he was gluten intolerant, but we had not realized it at the time, his appetite was poor and willingness absent. But we were able to get him to fall in love with broccoli by calling it "little trees" and by making sure it had lots of flavor. The red onion, garlic and sea salt help load this up with savory goodness while the roasting helps seal in these flavors and deliver them right into your kiddos! This recipe is a favorite from my mom, whom my kids call Mimi.

MAKES: 4 SERVINGS

24 ounces (675 g) broccoli and/or cauliflower florets

½ large red onion, diced

¼ cup (60 ml) avocado or olive oil

2 tbsp (9 g) minced garlic

1 tsp sea salt

½ tsp onion powder

Optional: ground black pepper

Preheat the oven to 400°F (205°C).

Combine all ingredients in a bowl and toss to coat evenly or place all ingredients in a large resealable bag, seal and shake to coat. Transfer contents to a large parchment-lined baking sheet and bake for 40 minutes, shifting the little trees midway. Carefully remove from the oven and serve once cooled slightly.

Give Peas a Chance Fritters

GRAIN FREE, GLUTEN FREE, DAIRY FREE, EGG FREE, NUT FREE, SOY FREE

Some kiddos love buttered peas without any fuss or presentation. My kids have even been known to eat them frozen as a snack (odd but true). But some littles just need the extra encouragement when it comes to greens. These fritters are crispy and feel like the perfect finger food when, in fact, they are the perfect green accompaniment to dinner!

MAKES: 4 SERVINGS

2 tbsp (30 g) + ¼ cup (60 g) ghee, avocado oil or olive oil, divided

1 cup (134 g) cooked green peas

½ cup (80 g) potato starch

2 tbsp (12 g) coconut flour

1 tsp garlic sea salt

¼ tsp onion powder

Ranch Dressing (page 173), optional

Preheat the 2 tablespoons (30 g) of cooking fat in a large skillet over medium/high heat.

Combine all of the remaining ingredients (minus the dressing) in a mixing bowl and stir or mix by hand until they are all incorporated evenly. Using your hands, take a small handful and form a patty or disc shaped fritter. Once formed, place your fritter into the hot oil and fry it until crispy, about 3 minutes per side. Remove the fritter and place it on a towel-lined plate to absorb excess oil. Repeat with remaining dough until it is all used. Serve warm. These are also great dipped in my Ranch Dressing.

FOR LITTLE HANDS: Allow your child to mix all of the ingredients in the mixing bowl and to help shape the fritters. If your child is older, this recipe may be followed start to finish under supervision.

Veggie Rice + Gravy

GRAIN FREE, GLUTEN FREE, DAIRY FREE, NUT FREE, EGG FREE, SOY FREE

Rice is a comfort food that spans all generations. It just feels like home. But when grain is out, finding that comforting side dish is tricky. My "rice" is veggie based so not only is your kiddo receiving comfort, you'll also be delivering some essential micronutrients!

MAKES: 4 SERVINGS

FOR THE VEGGIE RICE

4 large zucchini squash or yellow squash

1 tsp sea salt

1 tbsp (15 g) ghee, avocado oil or olive oil

FOR THE GRAVY

1 onion, any variety, chopped

8 ounces (225 g) white button mushrooms, chopped

1 tbsp (15 g) ghee, avocado oil or olive oil

½ tsp sea salt

¼ tsp garlic powder

¼ tsp onion powder

¼ tsp ground black pepper

1 (13½ ounce [370 ml]) can full-fat coconut milk

Optional: 1 or more tbsp (7 g) of tapioca starch

To make the veggie rice, spiral cut the squash on the thinnest setting. Or julienne it or mince it in a food processor. If you spiral cut the squash, then rice it by mincing it into small rice-sized pieces.

Place the cut squash into a colander and sprinkle the teaspoon of sea salt over it. Allow the squash to sweat out excess moisture while you prepare your gravy.

To make the gravy, saute the onion and mushrooms in the 1 tablespoon (15 g) ghee until tender in a small saucepan over medium/high heat for about 10 minutes. Sprinkle in the seasonings and pour in the coconut milk and stir. Bring mixture to a boil for just a minute or two then remove from heat and puree in a traditional blender or with an immersion blender. If you'd like a thicker gravy, you can make a slurry by removing ¼ cup (60 ml) of the gravy from the saucepan and stirring 1 tablespoon (7 g) of tapioca starch into the gravy. Reintroduce the slurry back into the gravy and stir once more.

To cook the veggie rice, heat 1 tablespoon (15 ml) of cooking fat in a large skillet over high heat and then gently transfer riced squash into the skillet. Cook over high heat, shifting contents regularly for about 5 minutes or until desired texture is reached. If you prefer more al dente cook less, or softer cook longer.

Once the veggie rice is cooked, remove it from the skillet and serve by spooning desired amount of gravy over it.

 FOR LITTLE HANDS: Allow your child to help spiral cut the squash and help chop it into rice sized pieces with a child-friendly knife. Older children can also help sauté the mushrooms and onion, while supervised, or even help operate the blender to puree the gravy.

BFF Brussels

GRAIN FREE, GLUTEN FREE, DAIRY FREE, NUT FREE, EGG FREE, SOY FREE

Oh, the age old joke about how terribly, awfully horrible Brussels sprouts are and why everyone who is anyone should toss them away at once! While sulfur-rich sprouts can create stinky memories of times past, these Brussels sprouts are so good you'll want to be best friends forever. My kids actually fight over these and force me to make extras! Oh the horror! Finally some Brussels that don't get "accidentally" fed to the dog!

MAKES: 2 SERVINGS

10 ounces (280 g) shaved Brussels sprouts

3 tbsp (45 ml) 100% maple syrup

3 tbsp (45 g) avocado oil, ghee or olive oil

1 tbsp (15 ml) spicy brown mustard

1 tsp garlic powder

½ tsp onion powder

½ tsp sea salt

Preheat the oven to 375°F (190°C).

Use a food processor to shave the sprouts if you don't buy them pre-cut. Combine all ingredients into a mixing bowl and stir to coat the Brussels well. Spread them onto a parchment-lined baking sheet and bake for around 20 minutes or until the pieces start to crisp. Midway you may shift the contents around to help facilitate more even crisping.

 FOR LITTLE HANDS: Allow your child to mix the ingredients in a bowl and spread them onto the baking sheet.

Zucchini Sticks

GRAIN FREE, GLUTEN FREE, NUT FREE, EGG FREE, DAIRY FREE, SOY FREE

Zucchini sticks are a great way to deliver greens to your little people by wrapping them in a light crispy exterior and dunking them into creamy dairy-free ranch dressing or warm savory marinara. Instead of a thick, greasy gluten-based crust, these have a thin crunchy coating that doesn't disappoint!

MAKES: 2 SERVINGS

Olive oil or avocado oil for frying

½ cup (120 ml) flax, coconut or other dairy-free milk

1 teaspoon garlic sea salt

½ teaspoon onion powder

½ cup (120 g) potato starch

½ cup (120 g) tapioca starch or arrowroot

2 zucchini squashes, cut into finger-width spears

Marinara or Ranch Dressing (page 173), for serving

Preheat the olive or avocado oil in a large skillet over medium/high heat. Pour the milk into one clean bowl, and combine the flours and seasonings onto a clean plate. Coat the zucchini spears in the flour mixture, then give them a milk bath before dredging in the flours once more. Tap off the excess flour and place into the hot oil. Cook on all sides until crisp, about 5-7 minutes, and then remove them with a skimmer and place them onto a towel-lined plate. Serve warm with marinara or my Ranch Dressing, or if serving later, reheat in the oven or toaster oven to crisp them back up again.

Superhero Smoothies

Let's be really honest for a second. Sometimes kids just don't get enough veggies or micronutrients into their bodies in a day. Sometimes grown-ups don't either! Smoothies are a great way to sneak in more of the good stuff, like greens, that some kids are resistant to eating. What's even better is the greens are often undetectable if done right!

In this smoothies chapter, I've given serious nutrition some fun names so that kids can pick their favorite and consequently get some great vitamins at the same time! The Orange Berry Banshee (page 134), Green Goblin (page 138) and Pineapple Phantom (page 145) are a few favorites that sound as entertaining as they are tasty!

Orange Berry Banshee

GRAIN FREE, GLUTEN FREE, DAIRY FREE, NUT FREE, EGG FREE, SOY FREE

The combination of citrus and berries is just the right one for sneaking in some Romaine lettuce! Your wee one won't even suspect the added greens!

MAKES: 1 LARGE SERVING

1 cup (130 g) frozen mixed berries
½ cup (120 ml) orange juice
½ cup (120 ml) sparkling water
2–3 hearts of romaine leaves

Blend all ingredients in a blender until puréed. If you prefer it sweeter, you can add 1 cup (240 ml) orange juice instead of ½ cup (120 ml) and omit the water.

FOR LITTLE HANDS: Allow your child to combine the ingredients in the blender or even operate the blender under supervision. Kids love power tools, and this is a great opportunity to teach safety in the kitchen!

Crantastic Trio

GRAIN FREE, GLUTEN FREE, DAIRY FREE, NUT FREE, EGG FREE, SOY FREE

This rich purple smoothie packs a tart + sweet punch for your little superhero. With only three ingredients, it's easy to whip up any time of the day for added nutrients. This one hides spinach without a trace!

MAKES: 1 LARGE SERVING

1 cup (130 g) frozen blueberries

½ cup (15 g) baby spinach

1 cup (240 ml) 100% cranberry juice

Optional: Stevia or local honey for added sweetness if the tart is too much

Blend all ingredients in a blender until puréed. This is a single serving so multiply it if you are feeding extra mouths!

FOR LITTLE HANDS: Allow your child to combine the ingredients in the blender or even operate the blender under supervision. Kids love power tools, and this is a great opportunity to teach safety in the kitchen!

Green Goblin

GRAIN FREE, GLUTEN FREE, DAIRY FREE, NUT FREE, EGG FREE, SOY FREE

Embrace your greens by sneaking them into this sweet combination of pineapple and banana. Want extra green? Add in a scoop of grain-free green powder to really intensify the color and nutrition!

MAKES: 1 LARGE SERVING

1 frozen banana
1 heaping cup (30 g) baby spinach
1 cup (240 ml) pineapple juice
Optional: green juice powder

Blend all ingredients in a blender until puréed. This is a single serving so multiply it if you are feeding extra mouths!

 FOR LITTLE HANDS: Allow your child to combine the ingredients in the blender or even operate the blender under supervision. Kids love power tools, and this is a great opportunity to teach safety in the kitchen!

Strawberry Superpower

GRAIN FREE, GLUTEN FREE, DAIRY FREE, NUT FREE, EGG FREE, SOY FREE

No hidden greens in this one but lots of Vitamin C for immune supportive superpowers! This one is naturally sweet so kids love it without the junk!

MAKES: 1 LARGE SERVING

1 cup (130 g) frozen strawberries
½ cup (120 ml) sparkling water
½ cup (120 ml) pineapple juice
Optional: 1 tbsp (7 g) grass-fed collagen

Blend all ingredients in a blender until puréed. This is a single serving so multiply it if you are feeding extra mouths!

FOR LITTLE HANDS: Allow your child to combine the ingredients in the blender or even operate the blender under supervision. Kids love power tools, and this is a great opportunity to teach safety in the kitchen!

The Great Caped Grape

GRAIN FREE, GLUTEN FREE, DAIRY FREE, EGG FREE, SOY FREE

This fun, creamy smoothie mixes two less likely sidekicks for a sweet delicious treat that packs in some great nutrients like resveratrol, polyphenols, Vitamin C and manganese too!

MAKES: 1 LARGE SERVING

2 cups (260 g) frozen grapes
½ ripe banana
⅓ cup (80 ml) full-fat coconut milk

Combine all ingredients in a blender and purée until creamy and smooth.

 FOR LITTLE HANDS: Allow your child to combine the ingredients in the blender or even operate the blender under supervision. Kids love power tools, and this is a great opportunity to teach safety in the kitchen!

Pineapple Phantom

GRAIN FREE, GLUTEN FREE, DAIRY FREE, NUT FREE, EGG FREE, SOY FREE

This yummy combo tastes like you've vanished from real life and landed on a tropical island! It's creamy and light and filled with just the good stuff!

MAKES: 1 LARGE SERVING

⅓ cup (80 g) frozen peaches
⅔ cup (160 g) frozen pineapple chunks
⅔ cup (160 ml) water
⅓ cup (80 ml) orange juice
Optional: 2 tbsp (14 g) grass-fed collagen

Blend all ingredients in a blender until puréed.

FOR LITTLE HANDS: Allow your child to combine the ingredients in the blender or even operate the blender under supervision. Kids love power tools, and this is a great opportunity to teach safety in the kitchen!

Breads 'N' Such

Oh carbs, we love thee. Practically from the beginning of time, breads, muffins and the like have provided comfort and satisfaction. With more and more kids experiencing gluten and grain intolerance, it's important to recreate old favorites so that children have safe options.

In this chapter, I've made sure that your children can experience a grain-free version of everything from Weeknight Paleo Tortillas (page 155) to Legit Sandwich Bread (page 148) for sandwiches, and from Mini Muffins (page 152) to Everyday Crackers (page 151). So if your family isn't quite ready to lettuce wrap all your proteins, that's OK, I got your back!

Legit Sandwich Bread

GRAIN FREE, GLUTEN FREE, DAIRY FREE, NUT FREE, SOY FREE, YEAST FREE

This recipe is the culmination of years of disappointment. I've wanted to crack the code on a real bread recipe that you'd never know is Paleo. This one is perfect for sandwich making, slicing thin and toasting. Your little one will never know this isn't real bread!

MAKES: 1 LOAF

¾ cup (96 g) cassava flour

¼ cup (40 g) potato starch or sweet potato starch

1 tsp baking soda

1 tsp sea salt

3 tbsp (28 g) psyllium husk powder (finely ground)

2 tbsp (12 g) coconut flour

7 eggs

3 tbsp (45 g) cooking fat of choice (olive oil, coconut oil, avocado oil or ghee)

1 tbsp (15 ml) apple cider vinegar

⅓ cup (80 ml) local raw honey

Preheat the oven to 350°F (175°C).

In one mixing bowl, stir together the dry ingredients. In another bowl, combine the wet ones, stirring well to combine. Keep them separate until right before you are ready to bake. Grease a toaster oven bread pan (this is a smaller size, around 7 × 3.75 inches [17 × 9 cm]) with cooking fat of choice.

Mix together the wet and dry ingredients and use an immersion blender to get a smooth consistency. Immediately spoon the batter into the bread pan and bake for 35–40 minutes. Remove from the oven when baked through and allow to cool for around 5 minutes before removing loaf from pan. You may need to use a butter knife to loosen the bread from the pan before removing.

Note: You may need to bake longer based on oven and altitude variations. Some have reported baking for around 50 minutes.

FOR LITTLE HANDS: Allow your child to mix the wet and dry ingredients in separate bowls and then combine them. With supervision, your child may also help use the immersion blender.

Everyday Crackers

GRAIN FREE, GLUTEN FREE, DAIRY FREE, EGG FREE, NUT FREE, SOY FREE

The word "cracker" loosely translates (from toddler language) to snack time. Kiddos love crunchy, bite-sized foods they can hold easily and self-feed. Oh, who are we kidding? Everybody loves a good cracker!

MAKES: 4 SERVINGS

½ cup (80 g) potato starch or sweet potato starch

¼ cup (30 g) tapioca starch

3 tbsp (18 g) coconut flour

1 tbsp (7 g) golden flax meal

1 tsp psyllium husk powder

¼ cup (60 ml) olive oil (or preferred fat)

¼ cup (15 g) palm shortening, softened

1 tbsp (15 ml) local honey

¼ tsp onion powder

½ tsp sea salt

¼ tsp garlic powder

Pinch ground black pepper

Preheat the oven to 350°F (175°C).

Combine all the ingredients in a mixing bowl until you can form a round ball of dough. Roll out the dough between two sheets of parchment paper until it is ⅛-inch (3-mm) thick. Next score the dough into the desired cracker size and shape with a pizza cutter or paring knife. Bake for 10 to 15 minutes or until crisp. Carefully remove the crackers from the oven and set aside to cool.

Note: These crackers are flaky and buttery and can be a little fragile. Be sure to let them cool completely, which will help them firm up nicely. Avoid rolling too thin for this reason as well!

 FOR LITTLE HANDS: Allow your little helper to combine the ingredients in the mixing bowl and form the ball of dough. Your little one may also be able to help roll the dough out between the parchment paper.

Mini Muffins

GRAIN FREE, GLUTEN FREE, DAIRY FREE, NUT FREE, EGG FREE, SOY FREE

Let's be really honest for a second here. Kids love carbs. Heck, grown adults love carbs. And there's nothing wrong with that, but there are not-so-great-for-you carbs and then there are better choices. This is a better choice! It's still that comforting starchy goodness that can be used for a treat but isn't overly sweetened or weighed down with gluten or grain. Plus you can even serve them up as cupcakes, so it's the muffin that wears many hats!

MAKES: 13 SERVINGS

½ cup (64 g) tapioca starch or cassava flour

½ cup (120 g) Sunflower Seed Butter (page 111) (you can also use cashew butter if nuts are tolerated)

½ cup (120 ml) pumpkin purée

¼ cup (60 ml) 100% maple syrup

3 tbsp (45 ml) avocado oil, olive oil, ghee or melted sustainable palm shortening

1 tsp 100% vanilla extract

Pinch sea salt

1 tsp baking soda

Preheat the oven to 350°F (175°C).

Combine all ingredients in a mixing bowl and stir to combine. In a greased mini-muffin tin, spoon about 1 tablespoon (15 g) into each of the reservoirs. Bake for 15 to 20 minutes or until an inserted toothpick comes out clean. Remove the muffins from the oven, allow them to cool slightly and then serve warm. They can be stored at room temperature in an airtight container, refrigerated or frozen for a later date.

 FOR LITTLE HANDS: Allow your little one to help stir the ingredients and fill the mini-muffin tin.

Weeknight Paleo Tortillas

GRAIN FREE, GLUTEN FREE, DAIRY FREE, EGG FREE, NUT FREE, SOY FREE

Whether your little one likes to eat them plain, rolled up with nut butter and banana or likes to feed them to their pet hamster, these grain-free tortillas are a hit and a half.

MAKES: 6 SERVINGS

1 cup (128 g) cassava flour

½ cup (120 g) ghee, avocado oil or cooking fat of choice

½ cup (120 ml) coconut milk (or preferred dairy-free milk)

1–2 tbsp (6–12 g) coconut flour

½ tsp sea salt or more to taste

Preheat a griddle or cast iron skillet to medium/high (stainless should work fine too).

Combine all the ingredients in a mixing bowl and use hands to combine well (starting with only 1 tablespoon [6 g] coconut flour and going up as necessary if you cannot roll dough into a ball with ease).

Pinch off ⅙ of the mixture and roll into a ball. Line the base of a tortilla press with a piece of parchment paper. Place the ball of dough on top of the parchment paper and then place a second piece of parchment paper on top of the dough. Press out the tortilla, but not too thin!!! It will crack if you make it too thin. Transfer the tortilla from the parchment to your heated griddle or skillet. Allow each tortilla to cook on one side for a few minutes or until it begins to bubble, then flip it over using a thin flexible spatula. Cook on each side until desired doneness is met, around 3 to 4 minutes per side is typical. Using a griddle will allow you to cook more than one tortilla at a time.

Note: If you do not have a tortilla press, you may either roll out the dough between two pieces of parchment paper or use the underside of a dinner plate to press it out (not too thin!) also using two pieces of parchment paper to prevent sticking.

Sweet Potato Slider Buns

GRAIN FREE, GLUTEN FREE, DAIRY FREE, NUT FREE, SOY FREE

These bite-sized beauties are as tasty as they are cute. Using a blend of sweet potato starch and flour, they are a perfect grain-, gluten- and nut-free option to house your favorite fillings!

MAKES: 6 SERVINGS

¼ cup (28 g) sweet potato starch or potato starch

¼ cup (30 g) tapioca starch

2 tbsp (14 g) sweet potato flour

3 eggs

2 tbsp (30 ml) maple syrup

2 tbsp (30 g) avocado oil, coconut oil, ghee or cooking fat of choice

½ tsp sea salt

½ tsp baking soda

Preheat the oven to 350°F (175°C).

Combine all the ingredients together in a mixing bowl and mix either by hand or in a blender. Pour ⅙ of the batter into a greased muffin tin cavity and repeat with the remaining batter. Bake for about 20 minutes or until an inserted toothpick comes out clean. Slice them horizontally once cooled. These pair perfectly with the Liver Lovin' Turkey Burgers (page 57).

Note: You can often find sweet potato starch at Asian and Latin markets. If not there, both the sweet potato starch and flour can easily be found online.

FOR LITTLE HANDS: Allow your child to measure out the ingredients (if old enough) and mix them together. Your child may also pour the batter into the muffin tin and help slice the slider buns (with a child-safe knife) once cooled.

Tortilla Chips

GRAIN FREE, GLUTEN FREE, DAIRY FREE, NUT FREE, SOY FREE

Was there ever a more loveable dip scooper-upper? Likely not! But with corn off limits, tortilla chips fade quickly into the queso sunset. Turn around that frown with my grain-free tortilla chips! They are corn free and extra crispy!

MAKES: 6 SERVINGS

Avocado oil for frying (or coconut, olive, sustainable palm shortening)

1 cup (128 g) cassava flour

5 pasture-raised eggs

1 cup (240 ml) dairy-free milk (coconut, flax, sunflower seed milk)

Pinch sea salt

2 tbsp (30 g) avocado oil, coconut or olive oil

Preheat enough frying oil in a large skillet to cover the bottom (a few tablespoons at least) over medium/high heat. Preheat the oven to 350°F (175°C).

Combine the remaining ingredients in a blender or mixing bowl and mix to incorporate well. Pour ⅙ of the mixture into the skillet and swirl the batter around until it fills the skillet and is very thin, like a crêpe. Fry the tortilla on both sides until cooked through and slightly crisped, around 3 minutes per side. Transfer the cooked tortilla to a parchment-lined baking sheet and slice into 8 equal-sized triangles with a pizza cutter. Repeat with remaining batter. Sprinkle additional sea salt if desired before baking. Now bake the chips up to 20 minutes or until crisp. Keep an eye on the chips as they will taste burned if too brown. Oven variability will affect cook time, so start with 10 minutes and go up as needed. Best served fresh, though they can be stored at room temperature overnight in an airtight container. They can be frozen as well. Toast to crisp them up again.

Note: If you are looking for an egg-free option, consider slicing my Weeknight Paleo Tortillas (page 155) into triangles and baking them at 350°F (175°C) until crisp, around 20 minutes.

FOR LITTLE HANDS: Allow your child to help mix the batter ingredients and slice the tortillas into triangles. Pouring and flipping the tortilla batter may be more complicated but may be possibilities for older children while supervised.

Pizza Crust

GRAIN FREE, GLUTEN FREE, DAIRY FREE, NUT FREE, EGG FREE, SOY FREE

It is actually illegal to be a kid and not love pizza, but for many kids, allergies prevail and pizza becomes off limits. Cheer your little one up by making this pizza crust and topping it with anything you desire! Be sure to try my Mini Pizza on page 50.

MAKES: 4 SERVINGS

¾ cup (96 g) cassava flour

¼ cup (32 g) arrowroot flour or tapioca

1 tbsp (6 g) coconut flour

1 tbsp (12 g) coconut sugar

½ tsp baking soda

½ tsp garlic sea salt

¼ cup (60 g) ghee, avocado oil or preferred cooking fat

½ cup (120 ml) dairy-free milk

1 tbsp (7 g) ground flax seed

Preheat the oven to 350°F (175°C).

Combine all of the crust ingredients in a bowl and knead by hand until you have a big ball of dough. Divide dough into 4 equal-sized balls for 4 mini pizzas or make 1 large crust. Roll out the dough between two pieces of parchment paper to desired thickness. If your dough cracks around the edges, just seal it back together with an oiled hand. I recommend making a thin crust (around ⅛ inch [3 mm] or less) with this one for optimal results.

Now bake the crusts for 8 to 10 minutes on each side. If making a large crust, flipping is more difficult, so one sided baking will suffice (bake 20 minutes total or longer if necessary.) Remove and spoon pizza sauce on top followed by whatever veggie/meat toppings you prefer. Return to the oven for another 5 to 10 minutes or until preferred doneness is reached.

FOR LITTLE HANDS: Your little one can help by adding the ingredients to the mixing bowl and combining them by hand. Your helper can also roll out the dough or decorate the pizzas with desired toppings!

Homemade Grain-Free Pasta

GRAIN FREE, GLUTEN FREE, DAIRY FREE, NUT FREE, SOY FREE

Store-bought wheat-based pasta is cheap and simple, but it often comes with a price of its own—inflammation, digestive distress and even behavioral issues in children. This recipe is simple to make at home and uses cassava flour, which resembles gluten-based pasta very closely. Make fettucine noodles by hand or run it through your pasta maker.

MAKES: 2 SERVINGS

8 cups (1900 ml) water

1 cup (128 g) cassava flour (not tapioca starch)

2-3 pastured eggs

3-4 tbsp (45-60 g) cooking fat (olive oil, avocado oil, ghee)

½ tsp or more sea salt

Optional: 1 tbsp (15 g) psyllium husk powder (finely ground)

Bring 8 cups (1900 ml) of water to a boil on the stovetop over high heat (add a pinch of salt if desired).

Combine all remaining ingredients in a mixing bowl. Using your hands, knead into a ball of dough. It should feel dense and glutinous once combined thoroughly. Use a bit of cassava flour to lightly dust an area to roll out your ball of dough. Roll out the dough with a rolling pin to desired thickness. Using a pizza cutter or straight-edged knife, slice your noodles as fat or thin as you like. Transfer them to the boiling water and let them cook until they float, just a few minutes. Using a slotted spoon, remove them from the water and transfer them to a strainer. Serve with desired sauce. To make macaroni noodles, see the photos below.

 FOR LITTLE HANDS: Allow your child to combine the ingredients and knead the dough. Your helper may also enjoy rolling the dough out with a rolling pin.

Knead the dough into a ball

Roll out pasta dough, slice off strips and roll into a hollow straw shape

Cut out noodles

Shape as you please

Crispy Taco Shells

GRAIN FREE, GLUTEN FREE, DAIRY FREE, NUT FREE, SOY FREE

Food textures can be quite the bargaining point when it comes to fussy kids. When they hate crunchy, they HATE crunchy; but when they want a crunchy taco, it better be crunchy or the party's over before it started. Crispy tacos make the Top 10 of kid-approved eats, but with corn missing from a grain-free lifestyle, this meal becomes more complicated. But this mom has a few tricks up her sleeve, and I've got a crispy shell that will fool the best of them! For this recipe, you're basically making thin crêpe-like tortillas which you then drape over a taco rack to bake until crisp. You can also bake them flat until crispy if you prefer a tostada to a taco shell.

MAKES: 6-8 SERVINGS

1 cup (128 g) cassava flour

5 pastured eggs

1 cup (240 ml) dairy-free milk like coconut or flax

1 tbsp (15 ml) olive oil

Pinch sea salt

Oil for frying

Preheat oven to 350°F (175°C).

Mix together the flour, eggs, milk, olive oil and sea salt. Whisk until smooth or blend in a blender. Heat a tablespoon (15 ml) of oil in a medium-sized skillet over medium high heat. Once hot, pour ⅙ of the batter into the skillet and swirl it around to spread it over the surface area of the skillet. Allow to cook for about a minute or two per side, flipping with a thin flexible spatula.

Remove the shell from the skillet and drape it over one of the slots on the taco baking rack. Add more oil to the skillet as necessary before cooking your next crepe. Once the taco rack is full (mine holds 4), bake the taco shells for about 20 minutes or until crispy. If you need a little longer, just keep an eye on them so they don't burn. Also watch that they do not slide off your taco rack as they begin to bake, if they do just quickly place them back on the rack.

These are best served fresh; if not they have a tendency to soften again but can be perked up by toasting them at 350°F (176°C) for a few minutes if needed. You can also use these to stuff all sorts of other proteins in like turkey lunchmeat or even tuna salad! Trust me they are super versatile!

 FOR LITTLE HANDS: Allow your child to whisk together the taco shell ingredients and even help drape the crêpes over the taco rack. Of course filling the cooked crispy taco shells is a great way to get your child interested in healthy food!

Hot Dog Buns

GRAIN FREE, GLUTEN FREE, DAIRY FREE, NUT FREE, SOY FREE

Finding a decent gluten-free hot dog bun is like finding a needle in a haystack. Finding a grain-free one is basically impossible. So naturally I had to make this recipe and decided to use my Legit Sandwich Bread (page 148) recipe as a foundation. Feel free to use it to make burger buns as well!

MAKES: 6 BUNS

6 eggs

3 tbsp (45 g) cooking fat of choice (olive oil, coconut oil, avocado oil or ghee)

1 tbsp (15 ml) apple cider vinegar

⅓ cup (80 ml) local raw honey

¾ cup (96 g) cassava flour

¼ cup (40 g) potato starch

1 tsp baking soda

1 tsp sea salt

¼ cup (36 g) psyllium husk powder (finely ground)

2 tbsp (12 g) coconut flour

Preheat the oven to 350°F (175°C).

Combine all of the ingredients and use either an immersion blender or conventional blender to blend the ingredients until there are no lumps remaining. Line a baguette bread pan with foil and grease it thoroughly. Spoon the batter into 6 oblong bun shapes and bake for 15 minutes. Remove from the oven and allow the buns to cool slightly before removing them from the bread pan and serving. Overbaking will make the buns more dense, so keep a close watch.

 FOR LITTLE HANDS: Allow your child to help blend the ingredients while supervised. Your helper may also help spoon the dough with assistance.

Sips 'N' Dips

If ever there were a toddler sport, it would have to be dipping finger foods. But if you've taken a gander at the ingredients in most store-bought condiments, it's pretty darn frightening. So let's keep it simple! I have rewritten the dipping code to include whole foods ingredients your kids will still love and you can feel good about too! The whole gang is there: ranch, honey mustard, guacamole and BBQ. Get your dippers ready!

In this chapter you'll also find homemade beverages to include in your child's repertoire. No more boxed chocolate milk needed, you are now armed with dairy-free chocolatey goodness with no junk. The Perfectly Pink Lemonade (page 182) is pretty awesome too, and no need for guilt!

Honey Mustard

GRAIN FREE, GLUTEN FREE, DAIRY FREE, NUT FREE, EGG FREE, SOY FREE

Honey Mustard embodies the perfect balance between savory and sweet and is really a very simple combination of ingredients. So why is it that the store-bought stuff has high fructose corn syrup? As a mom I find this a completely extraneous and nutrient-lacking ingredient. By making your own at home you can literally combine two ingredients you probably stock regularly and know exactly what your little one is dippin' into!

MAKES: 4 SERVINGS

¼ cup (60 ml) local honey, any variety

¼ cup (60 ml) organic yellow mustard (gluten-free)

Stir the two ingredients together until blended well. Store in your refrigerator until needed. Pairs perfectly with my Grain-Free Corn Dog Dippers (page 66).

 FOR LITTLE HANDS: Allow your child to stir the ingredients together. Older children can also measure the ingredients out prior to stirring.

Ranch Dressing

GRAIN FREE, GLUTEN FREE, DAIRY FREE, NUT FREE, SOY FREE

You don't have to be Southern to know that a good ranch dressing is one of the most life altering condiments there is! Fresh chives and dill combined with a good-quality mayo will get you well on your way to dipping heaven!

MAKES: 4 SERVINGS

⅓ cup (80 ml) Mayonnaise (page 189) or high-quality store-bought

¼ cup (60 ml) flax milk (or other dairy-free milk)

1 tsp minced fresh dill

1 tsp minced fresh chives

¼ tsp sea salt

¼ tsp pepper

¼ tsp garlic powder

¼ tsp onion powder

¼ tsp parsley

Juice from ½ small lemon

Combine all ingredients and stir well or pulse in a blender until creamy.

Note: To make this recipe egg-free, just find a high-quality egg-free mayo or make your own!

FOR LITTLE HANDS: This recipe is so simple your child may be able to make it from start to finish! Don't forget your kid-friendly knives and scissors to help slice lemons and cut fresh herbs!

Ketchup

GRAIN FREE, GLUTEN FREE, DAIRY FREE, NUT FREE, EGG FREE, SOY FREE

Most commercial ketchups leave a lot to be desired! And a lot of homemade ketchups still use bleached white sugar and often lack that authentic ketchup taste. This one omits the junk but tastes so great your little one will be dunkin' in no time!

MAKES: 10 SERVINGS

28 ounces (785 g) organic diced tomatoes

½ cup (120 ml) water

½ cup (120 ml) 100% maple syrup

1 tsp onion powder

1½ tsp (7 g) sea salt

¼ tsp finely ground black pepper

⅛ tsp celery salt

⅛ tsp mustard powder

6 tbsp (90 ml) apple cider vinegar

Pinch ground cloves

Combine all of the ingredients in a medium-sized saucepan and turn burner on to medium-high heat. Stir your mixture, and once it reaches a boil, reduce heat to medium and allow it to simmer, covered, for 45 minutes. Transfer the saucepan contents to a blender, being careful not to splatter the hot mixture. Puree for 2 minutes, transfer to a glass container, allow it to cool for 10 minutes and refrigerate until ready to use.

 FOR LITTLE HANDS: Allow your supervised child to help measure and add the ingredients to the saucepan and stir. If older, your child can help operate the blender as well.

Awesome Sauce

GRAIN FREE, GLUTEN FREE, DAIRY FREE, NUT FREE, SOY FREE

The name says it all! This sauce is awesome and a perfect condiment for everyone from little kids to your inner child. And if you can't make up your mind between ketchup, mayonnaise or mustard, then this is up your alley. Dip your heart out!

MAKES: 5 SERVINGS

¼ cup (60 ml) Ketchup (page 174) or high-quality store-bought

¼ cup (60 ml) Mayonnaise (page 189) or high-quality store-bought

1–2 tbsp (15–30 ml) yellow mustard

Optional: 1 tbsp (15 g) maple sugar

Simply mix all ingredients together and stir to combine well. This makes the perfect accompaniment to my Sweet Potato Bacon Tots (page 118).

 FOR LITTLE HANDS: Allow your child to mix the ingredients together. Older helpers can also measure the ingredients prior to stirring.

Easy Pizza Sauce

GRAIN FREE, GLUTEN FREE, DAIRY FREE, NUT FREE, EGG FREE, SOY FREE

Some store-bought pizza sauces can have loads of sugar and rancid oils in them. With just a few ingredients that you likely have on hand, you can make your own in just minutes!

MAKES: 10 SERVINGS

1 (14½ ounce [400 g]) can petite diced tomatoes or 2 medium-sized fresh tomatoes

1 tsp dried basil

½ tsp dried oregano

1 tbsp (15 ml) pure maple syrup or local honey (optional but recommended)

1 tbsp (12 g) maple sugar (optional but recommended)

1 tbsp (15 ml) olive oil

½ tsp or more sea salt

¼ tsp ground black pepper

½ tsp onion powder

1 tsp garlic powder

1 tsp dried parsley

Simply combine all of the ingredients in a blender and puree until smooth. You can use it right away, uncooked, or heat it on low in a saucepan. This makes a perfect companion to my Pizza Pockets (page 62).

 FOR LITTLE HANDS: Allow your child to help place the ingredients into the blender and if supervised, you might even let them help operate the blender, explaining of course all the ways to play it safe around kitchen equipment!

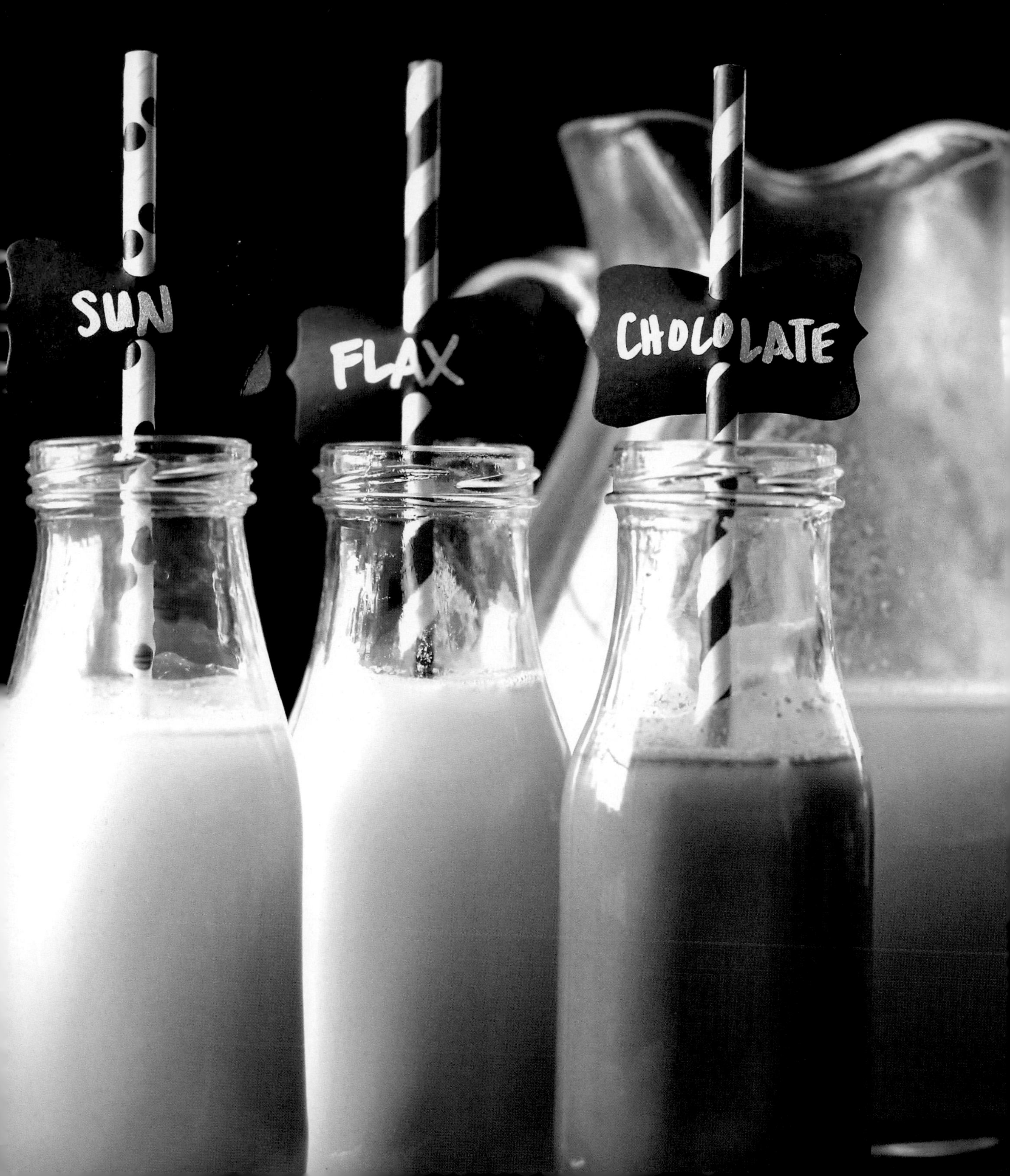
SUN
FLAX
CHOCOLATE

Chocolate Non-Dairy Milk with Variations

GRAIN FREE, GLUTEN FREE, DAIRY FREE, NUT FREE, EGG FREE, SOY FREE

Most people grew up understanding that a big tall glass of cold milk was part of a balanced meal. So what happens when dairy isn't tolerated well or must be removed from the daily routine? Luckily there are options, and they are simple enough to make at home if you want to avoid the added ingredients from store-bought varieties. You can also play around with coconut or nut milks if they are tolerated well.

MAKES: 4 SERVINGS (PER RECIPE, CHOCOLATE MILK IS A SINGLE SERVING)

FOR THE SUNFLOWER SEED MILK

1 cup (140 g) sunflower seeds (soaked for 2–3 hours minimum)

4 cups (950 ml) chilled filtered water

Optional: 100% maple syrup or local honey to taste

FOR THE FLAX MILK

⅓ cup (50 g) flax seeds (I prefer brown over golden)

3 cups (720 ml) water (plus 2 more cups [480 ml])

2 tbsp (30 ml) local honey or 100% maple syrup

FOR THE CHOCOLATE MILK

8 ounces (240 ml) dairy-free milk

1–2 tsp (5–10 g) organic cocoa powder

1 tbsp (15 ml) maple syrup

FOR THE SUNFLOWER SEED MILK

Drain the soaked sunflower seeds and empty them into a blender. Pour in the chilled filtered water and blend on high for about a minute. Using a nut milk bag (or clean, unused pantyhose) strain the liquid through the bag, leaving behind only the pulp. Now you may slightly sweeten your milk if needed. Store in a sealed glass jar in the refrigerator for up to a week.

FOR THE FLAX MILK

Combine flax seeds and 3 cups (720 ml) water in blender. Blend until thick and creamy then run the thick milk through cheesecloth or clean, unused pantyhose to strain seed particles. Once strained, blend 1½ more cups (360 ml) water plus honey or maple syrup to desired consistency. Flax seeds can create a thick milk, so add as much additional water as you'd like until you are content with it. Can be used right away or chilled for later use.

FOR THE CHOCOLATE MILK

Select 8 ounces (240 ml) of a dairy-free milk of your choosing. You may use the flax or sun milk options listed above or you may choose another milk like coconut or almond. Once you've poured the desired milk, add in the organic cocoa powder and then the maple syrup to sweeten. To dissolve the cocoa powder, either whisk vigorously or use a shaker cup with a lid to help agitate the mixture. A blender can be used too.

FOR LITTLE HANDS: Allow your child to help operate the blender under supervision or to help strain the milk through the bag or pantyhose.

Perfectly Pink Lemonade

GRAIN FREE, GLUTEN FREE, DAIRY FREE, NUT FREE, EGG FREE, SOY FREE

When summer rolls around, kids everywhere love hosting lemonade stands while sippin' on the sweet, tart goodness. But have you ever noticed the nutritional information on that canister of "naturally" sweetened powder? It's full of corn, soy and artificial colors, hardly what you want to feed your little people! My version has only lemons, water, honey, grass-fed gelatin for gut healing superpowers and a surprising pink addition that will give it color naturally!

MAKES: 10 SERVINGS

10 cups (2.4 L) water or sparkling mineral water

4 large lemons

¼ cup (60 ml) local honey or stevia to taste

⅓ cup (38 g) grass-fed collagen

3 tbsp (45 ml) elderberry syrup

Fill your pitcher or dispenser with the water. Slice the lemons and squeeze into the water. Add the honey and stir. Or you can use lemon-flavored stevia drops to taste. The collagen and elderberry syrup can be added at this time as well, stirring until dissolved. To make the lemonade extra tart, add more lemons. Serve right away or store in the refrigerator for up to a week.

 FOR LITTLE HANDS: Allow your helper to slice the lemons with a kid-friendly knife, squeeze the lemons and stir the lemonade.

Cheesy Dip

GRAIN FREE, GLUTEN FREE, DAIRY FREE, NUT FREE, EGG FREE, SOY FREE

In my neck of the woods, cheese dip is its own food group. And I know when I gave up dairy I was devastated by my loss of queso. So I can only imagine how hard it is for cheese-adoring kids to give up their favorites like creamy delicious dip! I made this delicious version so nobody has to sacrifice their beloved cheese dip!

The turmeric is mostly for color, but if you like turmeric you can go up to ¼ teaspoon. If you are sensitive to the flavor, start with just a pinch and go up from there.

MAKES: 4 SERVINGS

1 (13½ ounce [370 ml]) can full-fat coconut milk (or other dairy-free milk)

¼ cup (15 g) nutritional yeast

3 tbsp (45 ml) avocado oil, olive oil or preferred fat

1 tsp tomato sauce

¼ tsp cumin

¼ tsp garlic powder

¼ tsp onion powder

¼ tsp dry mustard, or less (you can start lower and work up)

¼–½ tsp apple cider vinegar (this provides a little tang)

Pinch paprika

¼ tsp turmeric

Sea salt to taste (I used about ½ tsp)

2 tbsp (15 g) tapioca flour

Combine all ingredients except for the tapioca in a saucepan. Bring to a simmer, whisking continually. Taste and add in more of the seasonings you wish or dilute with more milk if necessary. Once the flavor has been adjusted to your desired preference, make a slurry with 1 tablespoon (7 g) of the tapioca by removing 3 tablespoons (45 ml) of the cheese sauce from the sauce pan and mixing in the 1 tablespoon (7 g) of tapioca. Reintroduce the slurry back into the cheese sauce, whisking until it begins to thicken. If you'd like it thicker, use the second tablespoon of tapioca and make another slurry as mentioned above. Serve warm with my Tortilla Chips (page 159).

 FOR LITTLE HANDS: Allow your child to help whisk the ingredients in the saucepan, and take this opportunity to teach about taking precautions not to get burned.

Salsa

GRAIN FREE, GLUTEN FREE, DAIRY FREE, NUT FREE, EGG FREE, SOY FREE

I like to think of salsa as the next level of dipping for little ones. They might start out a little leery of all that kick but once they dive in, it's like new best friends on the spot. My Tortilla Chips (page 159) are excited to get busy, so make a batch and have them ready!

MAKES: 4 SERVINGS

13½ ounces (370 ml) diced tomatoes
¼ cup (60 ml) tomato sauce
¼ cup (40 g) red onion, minced
½ cup (8 g) chopped cilantro
¼ tsp ground black pepper
½ tsp sea salt
½ tsp garlic powder
¼ tsp onion powder
Pinch cumin
Juice from ½ lime

Combine all ingredients in a bowl and stir to combine. Feel free to adjust amounts of seasoning and add more or less as you'd like.

 FOR LITTLE HANDS: Allow your child to mix all of the ingredients and stir. Your child may also be able to help with the prep work with a child-friendly knife while supervised.

Mayonnaise

GRAIN FREE, GLUTEN FREE, DAIRY FREE, NUT FREE, SOY FREE

A good mayo is the foundation for so many fantastic dips and condiments. When you've got a clean mayo recipe in your arsenal, you can basically take over the world. Err, um, something like that!

MAKES: 12 SERVINGS

2 egg yolks
1 tsp apple cider vinegar
Pinch onion powder
Pinch garlic powder
Pinch mustard powder
½ tsp sea salt
¼ cup (60 g) coconut oil
¼ cup (60 ml) avocado oil
¼ cup (60 ml) light olive oil

Place the egg yolks and apple cider vinegar in a conventional blender or in an immersion blender cup. Blend to combine, about 10 seconds and then slowly begin drizzling the oils in, one at a time, blending continually to create an emulsion. It will get thicker and lighter. Keep adding the oils until they are all incorporated and your mayo is the texture of store-bought mayo.

 FOR LITTLE HANDS: Allow your child to help operate the blender while supervised and explain the importance of safety in using kitchen appliances.

BBQ Sauce

GRAIN FREE, GLUTEN FREE, DAIRY FREE, NUT FREE, EGG FREE, SOY FREE

Tangy and sweet, this BBQ sauce is perfectly paired with my Chicken Nuggets (page 49) or just about any other finger food that ever existed. You won't believe how fast you can make your own sauce—quicker than a trip to the store to buy a bottle in fact!

MAKES: 4 SERVINGS

½ cup (120 ml) Ketchup (page 174)
¼ cup (60 ml) water
⅓ cup (80 ml) 100% maple syrup
¼ tsp liquid smoke
½ tsp onion powder
½ tsp garlic powder
¼ tsp paprika

Combine all ingredients in a small saucepan and bring to a simmer on medium high. Simmer for 5 to 10 minutes or until thicker and less runny. Remove from heat and serve.

 FOR LITTLE HANDS: Allow your child to stir the sauce ingredients in the saucepan, and take time to explain the caution which must be taken when cooking over heat.

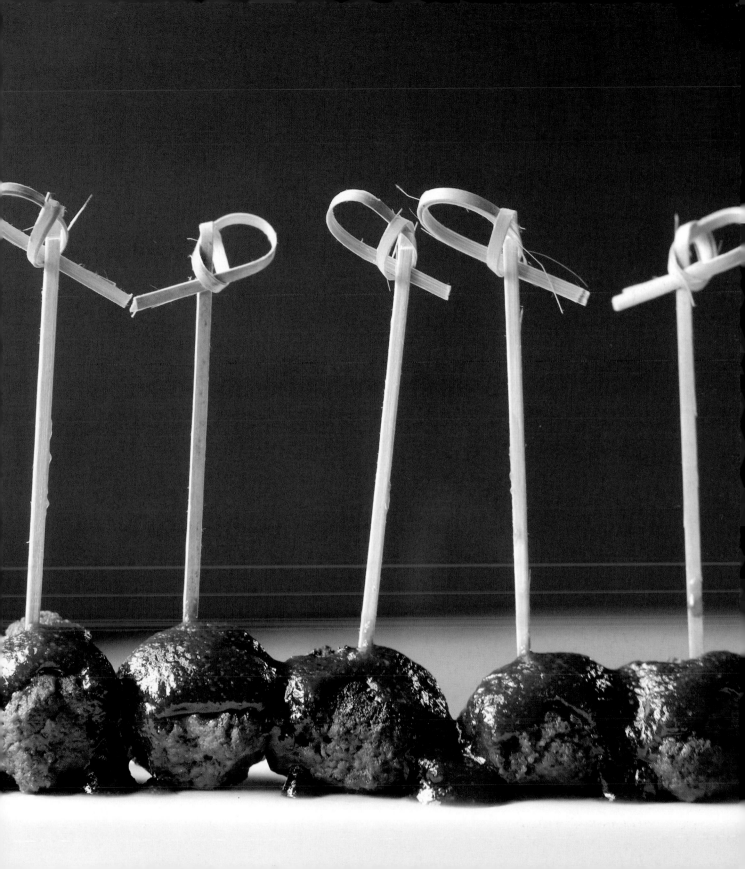

Rockin' Guacamole

GRAIN FREE, GLUTEN FREE, DAIRY FREE, NUT FREE, EGG FREE, SOY FREE

Avocado is such a great source of good fats and is a great first food, so why not keep it a part of your child's balanced diet? This guac takes just minutes and leaves out the jalapeño for developing palates.

MAKES: 2 SERVINGS

2 medium-sized avocados, scooped and pitted

½ a small onion diced

1 handful chopped cilantro

1 lime juiced

1 vine-ripened tomato diced

1 tsp minced garlic

½ tsp onion powder

½ tsp sea salt

¼ tsp freshly cracked black pepper

Combine all ingredients in a bowl and mash with a fork to combine. You can adjust seasonings to suit your preferences. Serve with my Tortilla Chips (page 159) or with plantain chips. Best if eaten right away but to store add extra lime juice to keep it from browning in the refrigerator.

 FOR LITTLE HANDS: Allow your child to mash all of the ingredients in a mixing bowl.

Dairy-Free Butter

GRAIN FREE, GLUTEN FREE, DAIRY FREE, NUT FREE, EGG FREE, SOY FREE

If your kiddo is anything like mine, you could spread butter on just about any food, savory and sweet, and they'd be overjoyed. Because I don't keep dairy in the house anymore and prefer not to use soy or rancid oils, I devised this butter recipe as my go-to creamy condiment (other than ranch dressing of course)!

MAKES: 6 SERVINGS

2 tbsp (30 ml) full-fat coconut milk

2 tbsp (30 ml) olive oil

1 tbsp (15 g) sustainable palm shortening, melted

2 tbsp (30 g) coconut oil, melted

3 tbsp (45 ml) avocado oil

½ tsp salt

To make the butter, combine all the ingredients in a blender and blend until creamy. Pour the mixture into a glass dish with a lid and freeze for 30 minutes (or refrigerate until solidified). Store any unused butter in the refrigerator.

 FOR LITTLE HANDS: Allow your child to help blend the ingredients while supervised.

Coconut Whipped Cream

GRAIN FREE, GLUTEN FREE, DAIRY FREE, NUT FREE, EGG FREE, SOY FREE

Whipped cream is the condiment that wears many hats. Perfect for dipping fruit or topping a dessert or hot beverage, whipped cream is the finishing touch to jazz up your dish. This one uses the rich coconut cream from full-fat coconut milk!

MAKES: 4 SERVINGS

1 (13½ ounce [370 ml]) can of full-fat coconut milk

1 tsp local honey, 100% maple syrup, coconut palm sugar, stevia or honey crystals (or more if preferred)

Refrigerate the coconut milk for at least four hours so that the cream will separate. After chilling, scoop out the cream into a mixing bowl. Using a hand blender, beat the coconut cream and the sweetener until it resembles whipped cream, about 5 minutes or more.

 FOR LITTLE HANDS: Allow your child to help mix the coconut cream with the hand mixer while supervised. If your child is younger you may help hold the mixer to stabilize it.

Hot Chocolate

GRAIN FREE, GLUTEN FREE, DAIRY FREE, NUT FREE, EGG FREE, SOY FREE

On chilly days, everyone loves curling up with a hot mug of cocoa. Those instant packets with the mini marshmallows are filled with frightening ingredients, and homemade versions still often use unnecessary dairy and refined sugars. I've been making this version since my children were very young and they still love it! Top with Coconut Whipped Cream (page 197) or homemade marshmallows from my S'mores recipe (page 206), and your child won't miss a thing!

MAKES: 3 SERVINGS

3 cups (720 ml) coconut milk, flax milk or almond milk

4 tsp (9 g) organic cocoa powder

¼ cup (60 ml) 100% maple syrup (or stevia drops)

3 tbsp (21 g) grass-fed collagen powder

Combine all ingredients in a medium-sized saucepan over medium-high heat and stir to combine. Bring to a simmer, stirring or whisking until all of the cocoa powder has been dissolved into the hot chocolate. Serve hot.

 FOR LITTLE HANDS: Allow your child to help whisk together all of the ingredients, and teach them how to be cautious while working over a heated surface.

Treats

One of the hardest things for me to have to tell my children was that they weren't allowed to eat the cupcakes at their friends' birthday parties. Not just the pizza, but the celebratory cake too! I learned early on that if I was going to enforce a healthier lifestyle for my kids, I better be prepared with an alternative for them.

So this chapter holds the recipes to help make your child feel like there is no missing out—that a birthday party can still be fun, and that your child is normal. I've got Cake Pops (page 217), Mint Chocolate Chip Ice Cream (page 218), Funnel Cakes (page 222) and Brown Sugar Cinnamon Toasted Pastry (page 213), all grain-free, refined-sugar-free and dairy-free. No more feeling left out!

Brownies

GRAIN FREE, GLUTEN FREE, DAIRY FREE, EGG FREE, NUT FREE, SOY FREE

Yummy, gooey, chocolatey brownies—they are great on their own or as part of a bigger plan, like a brownie sundae! You won't have to worry about allergens like eggs, dairy or gluten with this recipe. It's simple and delicious, and even better, your kids won't mind eating them one bit!

MAKES: 6 SERVINGS

½ cup (70 g) Sunflower Seed Butter (page 111)

3 tbsp (18 g) coconut flour

¼ cup (60 ml) pure maple syrup

1 tsp pure vanilla extract

1 tsp baking soda

¼ cup (60 ml) coconut milk

3 tbsp (15 g) cocoa powder

1 tbsp (7 g) grass-fed gelatin (the variety that congeals)

¼ cup (56 g) dairy-, soy- and refined-sugar-free chocolate chips

Preferred cooking fat for greasing baking dish

Vegetable-dyed sprinkles and homemade marshmallows (page 206), optional

Preheat the oven to 350°F (175°C).

Mix all of the brownie ingredients in a bowl and stir to combine well. Lightly grease an 8 × 8 inch (20 × 20 cm) baking dish with your preferred cooking fat and spoon the brownie mixture into the dish. Press the batter into the dish until distributed evenly. Bake for 10 to 15 minutes or until an inserted toothpick comes out clean. Remove the brownies from the oven, allow to cool and then slice and serve.

For fun, top with veggie-dyed sprinkles or homemade marshmallows after cooling.

 FOR LITTLE HANDS: Let your child pour the ingredients into the bowl, stir the brownie mixture or help press the batter flat into the baking dish. They can also help slice the brownies with a child safe knife.

Pudding Dirt in a Cup

GRAIN FREE, GLUTEN FREE, DAIRY FREE, EGG FREE, NUT FREE, SOY FREE

Remember this one? Chocolate pudding with crumbled sandwich cookies and gummy worms sprawling about…it's the novelty dessert that everyone must have at least once in their lives. I thought it would be fun to make this one without corn syrup, dairy and food dyes.

MAKES: 2 SERVINGS

2 Brownies (page 202)

½ cup (112 g) soy- and dairy-free chocolate chips, melted

¼ cup (60 g) coconut oil, melted

½ cup (120 ml) coconut milk

1 tsp 100% vanilla extract

Pinch salt

1–2 tbsp (15–30 ml) maple syrup

1 medium avocado, peeled and pitted

1 batch Gummy Worms (page 103)

Crumble the brownies into small pieces, like dirt. You can do this by sealing them into a zip top bag and crushing them with a meat mallet. Set the brownie crumbs aside.

Combine the melted chocolate chips, coconut oil, coconut milk, vanilla, salt, maple syrup and avocado and purée them in a blender until lump free. Spoon the mixture into two serving bowls, small flower pots or containers of your choosing. Sprinkle the "dirt," or brownie crumbs, on top of the pudding mixture in each of the serving cups.

Distribute as many or as few of the gummy worms as you'd like. Since they are fruit juice based and have gut-friendly gelatin, they are a healthy treat!

 FOR LITTLE HANDS: Allow your child to help blend the pudding ingredients, while supervised and also help crush the brownies into crumbs. Kids can also help fill the serving cups and decorate them with "dirt" and worms.

S'mores

GRAIN FREE, GLUTEN FREE, DAIRY FREE, EGG FREE, NUT FREE, SOY FREE

Oh man, S'mores are the best! Sweet marshmallows, gooey chocolate and crispy grahams. It's the treat trifecta, if you ask me. I created this recipe so that whether you bring the goodies on a camping trip, or just want to make them at home, you have the option without the grain and dairy.

MAKES: 4 SERVINGS

1 batch Graham Crackers (page 99)

1 bar dairy- and soy-free dark chocolate

Avocado or coconut oil for greasing

Cassava flour or tapioca starch for dusting

1 cup (240 ml) water, divided

1 cup (240 ml) maple syrup

1 tsp 100% vanilla extract

3 tbsp (21 g) grass-fed gelatin

2 tbsp (14 g) grass-fed collagen

Grease a small casserole dish (8 × 6 inch or 8 × 8 inch [20 × 15 cm or 20 × 20 cm]) with oil and dust with just a bit of cassava flour or tapioca starch.

Combine gelatin and ½ cup (120 ml) of the water in a mixing bowl. Bring the remaining ingredients to a boil in a small or medium saucepan over high heat. Allow it to heat to around 220–230°F (104°C–110°C) and then remove it from heat.

Slowly pour the heated mixture into the mixing bowl with the gelatin and water and start blending with a hand mixer on medium high. Continue slowly pouring until it has all been incorporated. Continue blending on high for about 10 minutes or until you have thick white marshmallow cream. Then quickly transfer the mixture over to the prepared casserole dish and using a floured or greased hand, pat the mixture into the dish. Allow it to set for 30 minutes or longer.

Slice the marshmallows and dust them again with more cassava flour or tapioca starch to prevent them from sticking to each other.

Assemble the S'mores by sandwiching ¼ of the chocolate bar in between two grahams. Add a marshmallow (sliced in half if necessary) to the s'more and serve. You can melt the choclate slightly if desired.

Note: these marshmallows are not good over an open flame or toasted. They will melt, therefore it is best to serve these as-is or let the chocolate melt them slightly.

 FOR LITTLE HANDS: Allow your older child to mix the gelatin mixture with the hand mixer. With hands-on supervision, younger helpers can also help assemble the S'mores once the marshmallows are set.

"Peanot" Butter Chocolate Chip Cookies

GRAIN FREE, GLUTEN FREE, DAIRY FREE, NUT FREE, EGG FREE, SOY FREE

This is one of my most popular allergy-friendly cookie recipes. In fact, I took it to my doctor as a treat for her son who has strict dietary limitations. She reported back that he absolutely loved them, and then told me I HAD to open a bakery! While I enjoyed the compliment immensely, I am mostly just glad to be able to share these peanut-buttery cookies with warm gushy chocolate chips with those kiddos who normally don't get such indulgences!

MAKES: 4 SERVINGS

⅓ cup (46 g) Sunflower Seed Butter (page 111)

⅓ cup (54 g) arrowroot flour

⅓ cup (80 ml) 100% organic maple syrup

1 tbsp (6 g) coconut flour

1 tsp baking soda

1 tsp 100% vanilla extract

¼ tsp sea salt

1 egg (optional)

⅔ cup (140 g) dairy-, soy- and refined-sugar-free chocolate chips

Preheat the oven to 350°F (175°C).

Combine the sunflower seed butter, maple syrup, egg (or omit) and vanilla. Stir well. Next add in the salt, arrowroot, coconut flour, chocolate chips and baking soda. Stir once more to combine.

Place small spoonfuls onto a foil or parchment lined baking sheet. Bake for 15 to 20 minutes, checking to prevent burning.

Note: If you want a thicker cookie that spreads less, add a second tablespoon (6 g) of coconut flour to your dough. Also, sunflower seed butter can turn green when baked. This is a completely normal reaction. Most kids are fascinated by the insides of their cookies turning bright green.

FOR LITTLE HANDS: Let your child help by stirring the dough or by placing the dough onto the cookie sheet before baking.

Double Chocolate Layer Cake

GRAIN FREE, GLUTEN FREE, DAIRY FREE, NUT FREE, EGG FREE

You know what makes me really sad? Knowing that a kid can't celebrate a birthday with a cake...or seeing that food allergies prevent a little one from feeling like one of the group. When I wrote this recipe for delicious layered chocolate cake with chocolate icing, I tried to picture those kids who typically can't partake. I am all for nutrients and limited sugars, but I also think it must be really hard to be a kid who is left out or unable to blow out candles on a birthday cake. So this is it! There are no eggs, nuts, gluten or dairy in this cake and yet it screams party, party, party! I hope it brings many memories for your little ones who have been feeling deprived in any way during a celebratory time!

MAKES: 8 SERVINGS

FOR THE CAKE

2 cups (128 g) cassava flour

2 tbsp (14 g) grass-fed gelatin (the kind that congeals)

5 tbsp (25 g) organic cocoa powder

2 tsp (8 g) baking soda

Pinch sea salt

2 tsp (10 ml) pure vanilla extract

1 cup (240 ml) honey or pure maple syrup

1 cup (240 ml) olive oil, ghee or avocado oil

3 tbsp (45 ml) applesauce

3 tbsp (45 ml) apple cider vinegar

FOR THE ICING

1 cup (225 g) dairy-free, soy-free chocolate chips

½ cup (70 g) sustainably sourced palm shortening

3 tbsp (45 ml) pure maple syrup

Pinch sea salt

1 tsp vanilla extract

Preheat the oven to 350°F (175°C).

In a mixing bowl, combine all the dry ingredients for the cake (cassava flour, gelatin, cocoa powder, baking soda and salt). Stir to combine and then add in the remaining ingredients except for the apple cider vinegar. Stir once more to combine all ingredients well. Last, add the apple cider vinegar and stir quickly.

Now divide the batter, which should have become more fluffy with the addition of the vinegar, into four 6-inch (15-cm) cake tins. Once you spoon the batter in, use your hands to gently press the batter into the tins.

Bake for around 10 minutes and then remove and allow to cool slightly.

While the cake layers are baking, make the icing. Melt the chocolate chips along with the shortening, maple syrup and salt in a double boiler over medium heat. Once melted, add in the vanilla extract and stir well.

Assemble the cake on a parchment-lined plate or baking sheet. Turn a cake layer out onto the parchment paper and spoon the liquid icing all over the top and down the sides of the layer. Repeat until all layers are stacked and spoon the last of the icing. Top with edible flowers, naturally dyed sprinkles or leave plain. Slice and serve once cooled and the icing hardens.

Note: Feel free to make extra icing if you'd like.

 FOR LITTLE HANDS: Let your child dump and mix the cake ingredients in the mixing bowl or even help spoon the icing over the top of the layers. It's okay to get a little messy!

Brown Sugar Cinnamon Toasted Pastry

GRAIN FREE, GLUTEN FREE, DAIRY FREE, NUT FREE, SOY FREE

Every child eating a Standard American Diet knows the toaster pastry well. The crispy pastry, sweet gooey filling and that icing that mysteriously never melts, even when heated. Needless to say, it's not a parent's dream food for their child, but it's a special treat that everybody loves! I've recreated this dish with zero refined sugar and added good fats to the grain-free goodness that children will love eating and grown-ups will love reminiscing about!

MAKES: 4 SERVINGS

FOR THE DOUGH

1 cup (128 g) cassava flour

⅓ cup (80 g) sustainable palm shortening, melted

1 egg

¼ cup (36 g) maple sugar

2 tbsp (30 ml) coconut milk (or more or less)

Pinch salt

FOR THE MAPLE CINNAMON FILLING

⅓ cup (48 g) maple sugar

1 tsp ground cinnamon

¼ cup (60 ml) dairy-free milk (coconut or flax)

1 tsp cassava flour

FOR THE BERRY FILLING

1 cup (130 g) organic frozen or fresh mixed berries

¼ cup (48 g) coconut palm sugar (optional)

FOR THE FROSTING

¼ cup (60 g) coconut oil or sustainable palm shortening, melted

2 tbsp (18 g) maple sugar

¼ tsp ground cinnamon

Preheat the oven to 350°F (175°C).

Combine all of the dough ingredients in a mixing bowl. You'll need to be able to form a ball of dough that isn't too dry or wet. If you sense that your dough will be too crumbly to roll out, add a bit more coconut milk. If it is too wet, sprinkle a little bit more flour until the right consistency is formed. Roll out the dough between two pieces of parchment paper until it is about ⅛-inch (3-mm) thick. Slice it into rectangles or squares; you should be able to make 8 rectangles per batch.

For the maple cinnamon filling, mix together the ingredients. The cinnamon maple filling will be a thick syrup which you can then place in the center of 4 of your dough rectangles. It's OK if it runs over a bit but try not to overfill.

For the berry filling, cook the berries and optional coconut palm sugar in a small saucepan over medium heat. Mash the berries and then simmer for about 5 minutes or until the mixture reduces and thickens. Spoon the filling into the center of each of four unbaked dough rectangles. Top with remaining dough and then use a fork to press the edges of the dough together all the way around (as pictured). Repeat with remaining pastries.

Bake the pastries for 15 minutes. Remove from the oven and allow them to cool completely.

While they are baking, mix together your ingredients for frosting. As the pastries cool, the frosting will transition from melted to slightly creamier, more opaque and thicker. At this time you can spread the frosting onto the cooled pastries, drizzle with remaining cinnamon filling and serve right away.

Note: These pastries can be toasted in the toaster if you prefer a warmer pastries, but the frosting will definitely melt off, unlike the original boxed version. If you want to warm them, keep the frosting separate and instead dip the warmed pastries into the room-temperature frosting.

Anything-But-Basic Vanilla Cupcakes + Bettercream Frosting

GRAIN FREE, GLUTEN FREE, DAIRY FREE, NUT FREE, SOY FREE

These delicious frosted vanilla cupcakes are great for birthday parties and can even made ahead and frozen for when your child attends a party with less than optimal treats. No need for any kiddo to feel left out with a recipe this simple to have on hand!

MAKES: 6 LARGE CUPCAKES OR MORE IF SMALLER

FOR THE CUPCAKES

¼ cup (60 ml) olive oil, ghee, melted palm shortening or avocado oil

½ cup (120 ml) maple syrup

6 eggs

1 tsp baking soda

½ cup (60 g) tapioca starch

½ cup (48 g) coconut flour

2 tbsp (20 g) potato starch

1 tsp vanilla extract

Pinch sea salt

FOR THE FROSTING

1 (13½ ounce [370 ml]) can of full-fat coconut milk, chilled

3 tbsp (45 g) ghee

3 tbsp (45 g) coconut oil, lightly softened

¼ cup (36 g) maple sugar, or more to taste

Optional: up to ½ cup (60 g) tapioca starch

Optional: vegetable-dyed sprinkles to garnish

Chill the can of coconut milk in the fridge for at least four hours.

Preheat the oven to 350°F (175°C).

Combine all of the cupcake ingredients in a mixing bowl or blender and mix well. Once smooth, pour the batter into six cupcake wrappers until almost full. Bake for 20–30 minutes or until an inserted toothpick comes out clean.

While the cupcakes are baking, use a hand mixer to blend the frosting ingredients. If you find the sugar separates from the fats in the frosting, add a bit of tapioca starch to absorb it. Beat the frosting until all of the ingredients are combined well. To make chocolate frosting, just add a few teaspoons of organic cocoa powder.

Allow cupcakes to cool completely. Then pipe or spread the frosting onto them.

FOR LITTLE HANDS: Allow your child to help mix the cupcake ingredients, pour the batter into the cupcake wrappers, mix the frosting ingredients and then pipe or spread the frosting. Little kids love helping prepare treats like this especially, so it's a great opportunity to explain the healthy ingredients you are using.

Cake Pops

GRAIN FREE, GLUTEN FREE, DAIRY FREE, NUT FREE, SOY FREE

Aren't cake pops just the cutest? Luckily, they are pretty easy to bake too and give you the perfect amount of treat without going overboard. I chose a vanilla base with a chocolate shell to get the best of both worlds!

MAKES: 15 SERVINGS

FOR THE CAKE POPS
¼ cup (60 g) olive oil, ghee, melted palm shortening or avocado oil
½ cup (120 ml) maple syrup
6 eggs
1 tsp baking soda
½ cup (60 g) tapioca starch
½ cup (48 g) coconut flour
2 tbsp (20 g) potato starch
1 tsp vanilla extract
Pinch sea salt

FOR THE CHOCOLATE COATING
½ cup (112 g) soy- and dairy-free chocolate chips
¼ cup (60 g) coconut oil

Preheat the oven to 350°F (175°C).

Combine all the cake pop ingredients in a mixing bowl or blender and mix until well combined and free of lumps. Once smooth, pour the batter into the bottom half of the generously greased cake pop pan, and then secure the top half of the pan. Bake for 15 to 18 minutes.

While the cake pops are baking, melt the coating ingredients. You may either microwave them in 30 second increments until completely melted and combined. Or you may melt them over a double boiler on the stovetop. To do this, bring 2 cups (475 ml) of water to a rapid boil over high heat and place a slightly smaller saucepan over the top of the one holding the boiling water. Place your coconut oil and chocolate chips in the top saucepan and stir until the mixture begins to melt from the heat of the boiling water below. Once melted, remove the saucepans from heat and set aside.

Remove the cake pops from the oven and gently remove the top half of the cake pan. Use a utensil if necessary to help remove them. Insert a lollipop stick into each of the cake pops. Dip one at a time until each is coated thoroughly. Place the cake pops onto a piece of parchment paper to allow the chocolate to solidify once again. If you want to decorate them further, you can add naturally dyed sprinkles at this time.

FOR LITTLE HANDS: Allow your child to help mix the cake batter or chocolate coating ingredients. You can also have your child help to dip the baked cake pops into the coating.

Mint Chocolate Chip Ice Cream

GRAIN FREE, GLUTEN FREE, DAIRY FREE, NUT FREE, EGG FREE, SOY FREE

A childhood favorite, from a certain ice cream shop, always made a regular day feel like a celebration. Fast forward to my own kids and the feeling remains the same. I've made this recipe without dairy or refined sugars and even made that pretty green color vegetable sourced!

MAKES: 4 SERVINGS

½ cup (120 g) coconut oil, melted
1 tbsp (5 g) cocoa or carob powder
1 (13½ ounce [370 ml]) can full-fat coconut milk
½ tsp real peppermint extract
¼ cup (45 g) fresh mint leaves
3 tbsp (45 ml) pure maple syrup
Handful fresh baby spinach (optional)

Pre-freeze your ice cream maker's insulated container. Or, if you do not have an ice cream maker, place a baking dish in the freezer.

Make the chips by combining the coconut oil and cocoa or carob powder in a shallow dish, and place it in the freezer for about 20 minutes, or until completely frozen.

In a blender or food processor, combine the coconut milk, peppermint extract, mint leaves and maple syrup. If you want a greener looking ice cream, add in the fresh baby spinach. Blend until the leaves are well combined and the mixture is smooth.

Remove the frozen cocoa/carob mixture from the freezer, and break up the thin, frozen layer into chips with your hands or a fork. Add chips to ice cream mixture.

If using an ice cream maker, pour mixture into ice cream maker and follow the directions for your machine. Serve when ready.

If not using an ice cream maker, pour mixture into a baking dish, and place it in the freezer. Freeze for 45 minutes. Remove the mixture from the freezer and stir it well with a rubber spatula, making sure to break up any hard, frozen sections. You can also use an immersion blender in your baking dish to do this. Place the mixture back in the freezer. Every 30 to 45 minutes, check the ice cream mixture and mix or churn it, until the ice cream is of the desired consistency. This should take about 2 to 3 hours. Freeze longer for a harder ice cream, or allow to thaw slightly before serving for a softer texture.

Note: using the coconut milk as a base, experiment with different flavors of ice creams.

FOR LITTLE HANDS: Allow your child to help blend the ingredients, while supervised, and then pour them into the ice cream machine. Your helper can also help break up the chocolate "chips" once frozen.

Strawberry Shortcake Bites

EGG FREE, DAIRY FREE, NUT FREE, GLUTEN FREE, SOY FREE

If your kiddo is more a fruity dessert lover, these Strawberry Shortcake Bites will really hit the spot. No eggs, nuts, dairy or gluten but lots of naturally sweet goodness!

MAKES: 8 SERVINGS

FOR THE CRUST

½ cup (48 g) coconut flour

1 tbsp (7 g) tapioca starch

1 tbsp (7 g) grass-fed gelatin (the variety that congeals)

⅓ cup (80 g) sustainable palm shortening, melted

1 tbsp (15 ml) pure maple syrup

Pinch sea salt

FOR THE FILLING

½ cup (75 g) diced strawberries

1 tbsp (15 ml) maple sugar

Coconut Whipped Cream (page 197), optional

Preheat the oven to 350°F (175°C).

Combine all the crust ingredients in a bowl, stirring well. If needed, you can add a bit extra liquid like water or dairy-free milk. This will be determined by the brand of coconut flour you use, as some are thirstier than others. You should be able to handle the dough and press it into the tartlet reservoirs easily. Divide the dough evenly among eight reservoirs in your mini tartlet pan. Press the dough into the tartlet molds, creating a dip in the center where for the strawberry mixture. Bake for about 8 minutes and remove from oven.

Now combine the maple sugar and diced strawberries in a bowl. Spoon the diced strawberries into the center and top with Coconut Whipped Cream if desired.

 FOR LITTLE HANDS: Allow your child to help chop the strawberries with a child-safe knife. Your little helper can also help stir the crust ingredients, fill the dough in the mini tartlet pan and help top them all with coconut whipped cream.

Funnel Cakes

GRAIN FREE, GLUTEN FREE, DAIRY FREE, SOY FREE

It's a fair favorite and a kid's best friend! Funnel cakes are a combination of elation and pure bliss on a plate. The light crispy curly design topped with that traditional sweet powdered sugar make funnel cakes not only delicious but also off-limits to grain-free eaters. This re-creation is even better than the original and won't leave behind a trail of nasty side effects!

MAKES: 6 SERVINGS

FOR THE FUNNEL CAKE
Coconut oil or avocado oil for frying
1 cup (120 g) tapioca flour
2 pastured eggs
2 tbsp (30 ml) pure maple syrup
2 tbsp (30 ml) avocado oil
Pinch of salt

FOR THE "POWDERED SUGAR" SPRINKLE
1 tbsp (12 g) maple sugar or coconut palm sugar
3 tbsp (24 g) tapioca flour

To make the funnel cakes, pour the oil into a saucepan to a depth of 1 inch (2.5 cm) and heat over medium high heat (using a small saucepan will help conserve how much oil you pour in).

Combine the tapioca flour, eggs, syrup, avocado oil and salt in a bowl. Stir until the batter is well combined.

Spoon the batter into a pastry bag and once the oil is shimmering (375°F–385°F [191°C–196°C]), quickly drizzle the batter into the hot oil, overlapping and making sure to not concentrate on one area (you are basically making squiggles and curlicues as you drizzle). Allow the underside to brown, around 1 minute, then use a flat slotted spoon to flip the funnel cake over and brown the other side. Remove the funnel cake from the oil and place on a towel-lined plate.

To make the sprinkle, combine the maple sugar and tapioca flour in a small bowl. Using a sifter, sprinkle the sugar mixture on top of the funnel cake. Serve hot!

 FOR LITTLE HANDS: Allow your child to help stir the ingredients in the mixing bowl. Older helpers may assist in frying the funnel cakes, but take care to be very mindful and observant of the hot oil. Sprinkling the "sugar" is another task any child may help execute as well.

Lunch Bunch

Multiple times a week I get asked, "What should I pack for my child's school lunch if I'm transitioning to a Paleo-oriented lifestyle?" In the beginning it can feel challenging, especially when mornings tend to be hectic and short on time. The good news is, school lunches can be as simple or as ornate as you wish to make them. In the beginning, if your children are used to sandwiches and processed foods, you may spend a little more time reconstructing lunches to "feel" like their old favorites. Perhaps using my Legit Sandwich Bread (page 148), baked in advance, to pack a sandwich will help ease the transition. Or maybe your little ones are just as content to have turkey roll-ups without the bread.

In this chapter, I've included some ways to incorporate colorful fruits and vegetables, as well as some better quality snacks and chips, in order to help school lunches be as enjoyable as they ever were without being too complicated. I recommend doing a little batch cooking on the weekends if you want to incorporate cooked foods. And of course, if you have leftovers from last night's supper, be sure to toss those into a thermos if your kiddos prefer a hot lunch. As mentioned in my tips and tricks for transitioning at the beginning of this book, get your children involved! Take them shopping and let them help pick some fruits and veggies they might enjoy having packed in their lunch so that they are invested in the process!

As your children are able to successfully make the transition, you may also be able to trust them to buy raw fruits and veggies from the cafeteria line to supplement what you send to school. This is something I've done with my children, and they love not only the autonomy, but also the opportunity to have the same experience at lunchtime as some of their friends. Don't fear the lunch! It might take a little time adapting, but in the end your children will be filled with nutritious foods you can feel good about.

Apple slices

"Cheese" Quackers (page 100)

Quesadilla (page 61)

Carrots and tomatoes

Sliced pears

Sweet potato chips

Pizza Pockets (page 62)

Sliced mini cucumbers

Pomegranate seeds

Mini sweet peppers

Turkey roll-ups

Pickles

Raw broccoli

Diced beets

Frozen grapes

Legit Bread Slice (page 148) with Awesome Sauce (page 177) and organic pepperoni

Grapes

Sliced tomato

Meat Pocket (page 58) with sliced bell pepper

Plantain chips

Zucchini

Butternut squash

Blueberries

Papaya

Liver

Avocado

Banana

Egg yolks

Broccoli

Beets

Sweet potato

Cavebaby's First Foods

Parents always want the best for their little ones, and when it comes time to introduce new foods, it can be as nerve-wracking as picking a baby name! Homemade or store bought? Organic or not? Which foods are safest, most nutrient dense? Baby led weaning foods or puréed? It can all be very overwhelming. Here I have a few easy-to-make, easy-to-store homemade baby foods that are accepted as safe, wholesome and easy to digest for earlier foods. Of course when choosing the best options and when to provide them, please consult your child's pediatrician or nutrition specialist.

These foods are included in the photo featured left. I selected them based on their nutrition profile, their common acceptance and baby's ability to digest them. Keep in mind there are many more foods I have not included which are also great options. When introducing meats, for example, there are a variety of fish that should be considered. And beyond the fruits and vegetables listed here, there are plenty more that can be added to the list. Also, some fruits and vegetables are considered safe raw, while others are best cooked in the beginning. For the list below I will notate whether they were raw or steamed; keep in mind that all of them were made to be as lump free as possible for beginning eaters.

Applesauce—Rich in Vitamins A and C, Folate, Potassium, Magnesium, Calcium. I make my applesauce in my pressure cooker. See recipe, page 76 and omit cinnamon if necessary.

Avocado—Rich in Vitamins A and C, Niacin, Folate, Potassium, Phosphorus, Iron, Magnesium, Calcium. Scoop out the raw flesh and purée it with a bit of water or breast milk until creamy. For older babies, cut the avocado into larger pieces instead of puréeing to promote self- feeding (good for baby led weaning too).

Bananas—Rich in Vitamins A and C, Folate, Potassium, Phosphorus, Selenium, Magnesium, Calcium. Bananas can be puréed raw after peeling. Add a bit of water or breast milk and purée until smooth. For older babies, cut the bananas into larger chunks instead of puréeing to promote self- feeding (good for baby led weaning too).

Beets—Rich in Vitamin C, Potassium, Folate, Manganese. Wash beets and boil them in water for about 10 to 15 minutes or until softened enough to blend. Purée in blender with a bit of water or breast milk if necessary. For older babies, cut the beets into larger pieces to promote self-feeding (good for baby led weaning too).

Blueberries—Rich in Vitamins C and K, Manganese. Blueberries can be boiled for a minute or two in a cup of water and then puréed with a bit of that same water or with breastmilk until smooth. Older babies can eat the blueberries raw and self-feed them whole (once ready).

Broccoli—Rich in Vitamins D, K and A, Folate. Steam broccoli and purée it with a bit of water or breast milk. Older babies can self-feed the florets if soft enough (good for baby led weaning too).

Butternut Squash—Rich in Vitamin A, Folate, Potassium, Calcium, Carbohydrates. Steam the squash until soft and then combine it with a bit of water or breast milk and purée until smooth. For older babies, cut the squash into larger pieces instead of puréeing to promote self-feeding (good for baby led weaning too).

Carrots—Rich in Vitamins A and K, Biotin, B6, Molybdenum, Potassium. Boil carrots in water for about 5 minutes or until soft enough to purée. Use a bit of water or breast milk to achieve a smooth texture. Older babies can eat the boiled carrots sliced into finger foods for self-feeding (good for baby led weaning too).

Egg yolks—Rich in Vitamins A, E, D and K, Folate, Iron, B6, B12, Calcium, Phosphorus. While egg whites can be problematic because of their allergenic proteins (to some), egg yolks are considered safer. You can hard boil the whole egg, pop the yolks out and purée them with a bit of water or breast milk until creamy. For older babies, cut the yolk into fourths, and allow baby to self-feed (good for baby led weaning too).

Liver—Rich in Vitamins A and C, Iron, Protein. Boil the liver for about 15 minutes in water. Purée it with a bit of water or breast milk until creamy.

Papaya—Rich in Vitamin C, Folate and Papain, a digestive enzyme. Steam papaya just until soft and then purée in a bit of water or breast milk until smooth. For older babies, cut the papaya into larger pieces (raw) to promote self-feeding (good for baby led weaning too)!

Sweet Potatoes—Rich in Vitamins A and C, Folate, Potassium, Sodium, Selenium, Phosphorous, Magnesium, Calcium. Steam or bake until soft then scoop out the flesh and purée with a bit of water or breast milk until smooth. For older babies, cut the sweet potatoes into larger pieces to promote self-feeding (good for baby led weaning too).

Zucchini—Rich in Vitamins A and C, Magnesium, Folate, Potassium, Copper, Phosphorus. Zucchini can be puréed raw and needs no additional liquid because of its water content. Older babies can eat finger food–sized slices of zucchini, cooked or raw, to promote self-feeding (good for baby led weaning too).

Acknowledgments

To my littles—Noah, Sadie and Stella: For tolerating my apparent book-writing addiction without abandoning me forever and for eating my recipes even before they've been "optimized!"

To my husband, Ben: For always cleaning up the kitchen after my long days of experimentation and for embracing my crazy creative side even when it's not always understood completely!

To my readers: For always supporting me, lifting me up and helping me run off trolls when they try to break up the party.

To all the kiddos near and far: For your intolerances and your need to feel normal. I would never have been so inspired to write these for you if I hadn't seen and experienced how hard it is to be different.

To my bloggy friends: For listening to me freak out when I don't think I could possibly record, write or photograph another recipe.

To my neighbors: For eating all my experiments and letting me know when they were "book-worthy" recipes.

To Kristen: For lending me your most fabulous kitchen so that we could nail the perfect cover photo.

To Page Street Publishing: For taking a THIRD chance on this girl and believing that my work is worthy enough to revisit again and again (and again).

To Dr. Freeman: For helping guide me from my very worst to assisting me in maximizing my health in every aspect. Thank you for writing the foreword to this book and for being there every step of the way.

About the Author

Jennifer is the voice and whole foodist behind the popular food blog Predominantly Paleo and bestselling author of *Down South Paleo* and *The New Yiddish Kitchen*. After being diagnosed with several autoimmune conditions and chronic infections, including Lyme disease, Jennifer became gravely ill and mostly housebound. When traditional medical treatments failed to help, Jennifer turned to food for healing. Removing grain, dairy and refined sugars and eating "predominantly Paleo," she started reclaiming her life, one whole food at a time. As a wife and mother of three, Jennifer hopes to instill healthy habits in her children now in hopes of creating wellness for a lifetime.

Index

Note: Page numbers in italics indicate photographs.

A

Allergy-Friendly Waffles, 18, *19*

almond milk, 198

Animal Crackers, 104, *105*

Anything-But-Basic Vanilla Cupcakes + Bettercream Frosting, 214, *215*

Apple Cars + Caramel Dip, *114,* 115

apple cider vinegar, 185, 189

apples

 Apple Cars + Caramel Dip, 115

 Cinnamon Applesauce, 76

applesauce, 232

arrowroot, 80

arrowroot flour

 "Peanot" Butter Chocolate Chip Cookies, 209

 Pizza Crust, 160

avocados, 193, 232

Awesome Sauce, *176, 177*

B

baby foods, 231–32

backup plans, 12

bacon, 118

Banana Pudding, *74, 75*

bananas, 232

 Banana Pudding, 75

 The Great Caped Grape, 142

 Green Goblin, 138

basil

 Easy Pizza Sauce, 178

 Mini Pizzas, 50

BBQ Sauce, 190, *191*

beef

 Bone Broth, 72

 Glazed Grain-Free Meatloaf + Crispy Onion Topping, 42

 Grain-Free Corn Dog Dippers, 66

 Meat Pockets, 58

 Veggie Spaghetti + Meatballs, 45

beets, 232

berries. *See also specific berries*

 Apple Cars + Caramel Dip, 115

 Brown Sugar Cinnamon Toasted Pastry, 213

 Orange Berry Banshee, 133

beverages, 169, 180. *See also Smoothies*

 Chocolate Non-Dairy Milk with Variations, *180,* 181

Hot Chocolate, 198, *199*

 Perfectly Pink Lemonade, 182, *183*

BFF Brussels, *128, 129*

blackberries, 25

blueberries, 25, 232

 Apple Cars + Caramel Dip, 115

 Crantastic Trio, 137

Bone Broth, 72, *73*

breads, 147–67

 Hot Dog Buns, *166,* 167

 Legit Sandwich Bread, 148, *149*

 Mini Muffins, 152, *153*

 Pizza Crust, 160, *161*

 Sweet Potato Slider Buns, 156, *157*

 Tortilla Chips, *158,* 159

 Weeknight Paleo Tortillas, *154,* 155

breakfast dishes, 17–39

 Allergy-Friendly Waffles, 18, *19*

 Cinnamon Maple Plantains, *32,* 33

 Cocoa 'N' Oatmeal, 30, *31*

 Egg in a Hole, *20,* 21

 French Toast Sticks, 26, *27*

 Fruit Kabobs + Dairy-Free Dip, *24,* 25

 Grain- + Nut-Free Granola, 22, *23*

 Green Eggs + Ham Roll Ups, 38, *39*

 Pale-O's Cereal, *36,* 37

 Sausage Quiche, *28,* 29

 Silver Dollar Chocolate Chip Pancakes, 34, *35*

broccoli, 122, 232

Brownies, 202, *203*

 Pudding Dirt in a Cup, 205

Brown Sugar Cinnamon Toasted Pastry, *212,* 213

Brussels sprouts, 129

butter, dairy-free, 194, *195*

butternut squash, 232

C

Cake Pops, *216, 217*

cakes

 Anything-But-Basic Vanilla Cupcakes + Bettercream Frosting, 214

 Cake Pops, 217

 Double Chocolate Layer Cake, 210

 Funnel Cakes, 222

 Strawberry Shortcake Bites, 221

cantaloupe, 25

carob powder, 218

carrots, 232

 Chicken Zoodle Soup, 54

Meat Pockets, 58

cashews

 Grilled Cheese, 53

 Mini Pizzas, 50

cassava flour

 Brown Sugar Cinnamon Toasted Pastry, 213

 "Cheese" Quackers, 100

 Crispy Taco Shells, 164

 Double Chocolate Layer Cake, 210

 Homemade Grain-Free Pasta, 163

 Hot Dog Buns, 167

 Legit Sandwich Bread, 148

 Mac 'N' "Cheese", 65

 Mini Muffins, 152

 Paleo Piggies, 112

 Pale-O's Cereal, 37

 Pizza Crust, 160

 S'mores, 206

 Soft Pretzels, 107

 Sweet Potato Bacon Tots, 118

 Tortilla Chips, 159

 Vanilla Wafers, 95

 Weeknight Paleo Tortillas, 155

cauliflower, 122

celery

 Chicken Zoodle Soup, 54

 Critters on Logs + Homemade Sunflower Seed Butter, 111

cereal

 Cocoa 'N' Oatmeal, 30

 Grain- + Nut-Free Granola, 22, *23*

 Pale-O's Cereal, 36, *37*

"Cheese" Quackers, 100, *101*

Cheesy Dip, *184,* 185

cherries, 111

chicken

 Bone Broth, 72

 Chicken Nuggets, 49

 Chicken Zoodle Soup, 54

 Liver Lovin' Turkey Burger Sliders, 57

Chicken Nuggets, *48,* 49

Chicken Zoodle Soup, 54, *55*

chips, *158, 159*

chives

 Ladybug Veggie Bites, 88

 Ranch, 173

 Teriyaki Meatballs + Daikon Noodles, 69

chocolate

 Brownies, 202

 Cake Pops, 217

Chocolate Non-Dairy Milk with
Variations, *180*
Critters on Logs + Homemade Sunflower
Seed Butter, 111
Double Chocolate Layer Cake, 210
Hot Chocolate, 198
Mint Chocolate Chip Ice Cream, 218
Pudding Dirt in a Cup, 205
S'mores, 206
chocolate chips
Brownies, 202
Cake Pops, 217
Critters on Logs + Homemade Sunflower
Seed Butter, 111
Double Chocolate Layer Cake, 210
Mint Chocolate Chip Ice Cream, 218
Pudding Dirt in a Cup, 205
Chocolate Non-Dairy Milk with Variations,
180, 181
cilantro, 29
Rockin' Guacamole, 193
Salsa, 186
cinnamon
Brown Sugar Cinnamon Toasted Pastry,
213
Cinnamon Applesauce, 76
Cinnamon Maple Plantains, 33
Monkey Toes (Filled Dates), 108
Cinnamon Applesauce, 76, *77*
Cinnamon Maple Plantains, 32, *32*
Cocoa 'N' Oatmeal, 30, *31*
cocoa powder
Brownies, 202
Chocolate Non-Dairy Milk with
Variations, 181
Cocoa 'N' Oatmeal, 30
Double Chocolate Layer Cake, 210
Hot Chocolate, 198
Mint Chocolate Chip Ice Cream, 218
coconut, 22
Critters on Logs + Homemade Sunflower
Seed Butter, 111
Lala Truffles, 92
coconut cream, 96
coconut flour, 18, 22
Animal Crackers, 104
Anything-But-Basic Vanilla Cupcakes +
Bettercream Frosting, 214
Brownies, 202
Cake Pops, 217
Everyday Crackers, 151
Give Peas a Chance Fritters, 125
Graham Crackers, 99
Grain-Free Corn Dog Dippers, 66
Hot Dog Buns, 167

Legit Sandwich Bread, 148
Pale-O's Cereal, 37
"Peanot" Butter Chocolate Chip Cookies,
209
Pizza Crust, 160
Silver Dollar Chocolate Chip Pancakes, 34
Soft Pretzels, 107
Strawberry Shortcake Bites, 221
Weeknight Paleo Tortillas, 155
coconut milk, 18, 26
Apple Cars + Caramel Dip, 115
Brownies, 202
Brown Sugar Cinnamon Toasted Pastry,
213
"Cheese" Quackers, 100
Cheesy Dip, 185
Coconut Whipped Cream, 197
Crispy Taco Shells, 164
Critters on Logs + Homemade Sunflower
Seed Butter, 111
Dairy-Free Butter, 194
Dairy-Free Coconut Yogurt, 80
The Great Caped Grape, 142
Hot Chocolate, 198
Mint Chocolate Chip Ice Cream, 218
Pale-O's Cereal, 37
Papaya"sick"les with Electrolytes, 83
Pudding Dirt in a Cup, 205
Silver Dollar Chocolate Chip Pancakes, 34
Tortilla Chips, 159
Weeknight Paleo Tortillas, 155
coconut oil
Critters on Logs + Homemade Sunflower
Seed Butter, 111
Dairy-Free Butter, 194
Mint Chocolate Chip Ice Cream, 218
Pale-O's Cereal, 37
Pudding Dirt in a Cup, 205
coconut sugar, 222
Pizza Crust, 160
Coconut Whipped Cream, *196, 197*
cod, 46
condiments, 169–79
Anything-But-Basic Vanilla Cupcakes +
Bettercream Frosting, 214
Awesome Sauce, *176,* 177
BBQ Sauce, 190, *191*
Cheesy Dip, *184,* 185
Coconut Whipped Cream, *196,* 197
Dairy-Free Butter, 194, *195*
Easy Pizza Sauce, 178, *179*
Honey Mustard, 170, *171*
Ketchup, 174, 1*75*
Mayonnaise, *188,* 189
Ranch, *172, 173*

Rockin' Guacamole, *192,* 193
Salsa, 186, *187*
cookies
Graham Crackers, 99
"Peanot" Butter Chocolate Chip Cookies,
209
Vanilla Wafers, 95
crackers
"Cheese" Quackers, 100
Everyday Crackers, *150,* 151
Graham Crackers, 99
cranberries, 111
cranberry juice, 137
Crantastic Trio, *136, 137*
Crispy Sweet Potato Fish Sticks, 46, *47*
Crispy Taco Shells, 164, *165*
Critters on Logs + Homemade Sunflower Seed
Butter, *110,* 111
cucumbers, 88
cumin, 186
cupcakes, 214

D
Dairy-Free Butter, 194, *195*
Dairy-Free "Cheese"
Ham + "Cheese" Quesadillas, 61
Pizza Pockets, 62
Dairy-Free Coconut Yogurt, 80, *81*
dates
Lala Truffles, 92
Monkey Toes (Filled Dates), 108
dill, 173
dips, 185. *See also condiments*
Double Chocolate Layer Cake, 210, *211*
dressings, Ranch, 173

E
Easy Pizza Sauce, 62, 178, *179*
educating kids, 13
Egg in a Hole, *20, 21*
eggs
Egg in a Hole, *20, 21*
egg yolks, 232
French Toast Sticks, 26
Funnel Cakes, 222
Green Eggs + Ham Roll Ups, 38, *39*
Homemade Grain-Free Pasta, 163
Mayonnaise, 189
Sausage Quiche, 29
Soft Pretzels, 107
Tortilla Chips, 159
elderberry syrup, 182
electrolytes, 83
Everyday Crackers, *150,* 151

F
favorites, recreating, 12–13
first foods, 231–32
fish sticks, 46
flax meal
    Everyday Crackers, 151
    Paleo Piggies, 112
Flax Milk, 181
    Brown Sugar Cinnamon Toasted Pastry, 213
    Crispy Taco Shells, 164
    Hot Chocolate, 198
    Ranch, 173
    Tortilla Chips, 159
flax seeds, 22, 99
Flu Season Gummies, 84, *85*
French Toast Sticks, 26, *27*
frosting, 214
fruit, 25. *See also specific fruits*
fruit juice, 103. *See also specific juices*
Fruit Kabobs + Dairy-Free Dip, *24*, 25
fun, 15
Funnel Cakes, 222, *223*

G
garlic, 122
Ginger Chews, *78, 79*
ginger root, 79
Give Peas a Chance Fritters, *124*, 125
Glazed Grain-Free Meatloaf + Crispy Onion
    Topping, 42, *43*
gluten, 10
Graham Crackers, *98, 99*, 206
Grain- + Nut-Free Granola, 22, *23*
Grain-Free Corn Dog Dippers, 66, *67*
granola
    Cocoa 'N' Oatmeal, 30
    Grain- + Nut-Free Granola, 22, *23*
grape juice, Great Grape Gummies, 91
grapes, The Great Caped Grape, 142
The Great Caped Grape, 142, *143*
Great Grape Gummies, *90*, 91
Green Eggs + Ham Roll Ups, 38, *39*
Green Goblin, 138, *139*
Grilled Cheese, *52*, 53
guacamole, 193
gummies
    Flu Season Gummies, 84
    Great Grape Gummies, 91
    Gummy Worms, 103
    Orange Dreamysicle Gummies, 96
Gummy Worms, *102*, 103

H
ham
    Green Eggs + Ham Roll Ups, 38, *39*
    Ham + "Cheese" Quesadillas, *60*, 61
healing foods, 71–85
    Banana Pudding, *74*, 75
    Bone Broth, 72, *73*
    Cinnamon Applesauce, 76, *77*
    Dairy-Free Coconut Yogurt, 80, *81*
    Flu Season Gummies, 84, *85*
    Ginger Chews, *78*, 79
    Papaya"sick"les with Electrolytes, *82*, 83
Homemade Grain-Free Pasta, *162, 163*
honey, 22, 25
    Animal Crackers, 104
    Coconut Whipped Cream, 197
    Double Chocolate Layer Cake, 210
    Ginger Chews, 79
    Honey Mustard, 170
    Hot Dog Buns, 167
    Orange Dreamysicle Gummies, 96
    Paleo Piggies, 112
    Perfectly Pink Lemonade, 182
    Vanilla Wafers, 95
honeydew, 25
Honey Mustard, 170, *171*
Hot Chocolate, 198, 1*99*
Hot Dog Buns, *166*, 167

I
ice cream, 218
involving kids, 13

K
Ketchup, 174, *175*, 177, *190*
kids, involving and educating, 13

L
Ladybug Veggie Bites, 88, *89*
Lala Truffles, 92, *93*
Legit Sandwich Bread, 148, *149*
lemons, 182
lettuce, 133
limes, 186, 193
liver, 232
Liver Lovin' Turkey Burger Sliders, *56*, 57
lunches, packing, 13, *224–30*

M
Mac 'N' "Cheese," *64, 65*
main dishes, 41–69
    Chicken Nuggets, *48*, 49
    Chicken Zoodle Soup, 54, *55*

Crispy Sweet Potato Fish Sticks, 46, *47*
    Glazed Grain-Free Meatloaf + Crispy
        Onion Topping, 42, *43*
    Grain-Free Corn Dog Dippers, 66
    Grilled Cheese, *52*, 53
    Ham + "Cheese" Quesadillas, *60*, 61, *61*
    Liver Lovin' Turkey Burger Sliders, *56*, 57
    Mac 'N' "Cheese", *64*, 65
    Meat Pockets, 58, *59*
    Mini Pizzas, 50, *51*
    Pizza Pockets, 62, *63*
    Teriyaki Meatballs + Daikon Noodles,
        68, 69
    Veggie Spaghetti + Meatballs, *44*, 45
maple sugar
    Anything-But-Basic Vanilla Cupcakes +
        Bettercream Frosting, 214
    Brown Sugar Cinnamon Toasted Pastry,
        213
    Strawberry Shortcake Bites, 221
maple syrup, 18, 26
    Apple Cars + Caramel Dip, 115
    Banana Pudding, 75
    BBQ Sauce, 190
    BFF Brussels, 129
    Brownies, 202
    Cake Pops, 217
    Chocolate Non-Dairy Milk with
        Variations, 181
    Cinnamon Maple Plantains, 33
    Critters on Logs + Homemade Sunflower
        Seed Butter, 111
    Dairy-Free Coconut Yogurt, 80
    Double Chocolate Layer Cake, 210
    Funnel Cakes, 222
    Graham Crackers, 99
    Great Grape Gummies, 91
    Hot Chocolate, 198
    Ketchup, 174
    Mini Muffins, 152
    Mint Chocolate Chip Ice Cream, 218
    Pale-O's Cereal, 37
    "Peanot" Butter Chocolate Chip Cookies,
        209
    Pudding Dirt in a Cup, 205
    Silver Dollar Chocolate Chip Pancakes, 34
    S'mores, 206
    Soft Pretzels, 107
    Strawberry Shortcake Bites, 221
    Sweet Potato Slider Buns, 156
Mayonnaise, 173, *188*, 189
meatloaf, 42
Meat Pockets, 58, *59*
Mimi's Little Veggie Trees, 122, *123*

Mini Muffins, 152, *153*
Mini Pizzas, 50, *51*
Mint Chocolate Chip Ice Cream, 218, *219*
molasses, 99
Monkey Toes (Filled Dates), 108, *109*
muffins, 152
mushrooms, 126
mustard, 170
    Cheesy Dip, 185
    Honey Mustard, 170

N
no junk kitchen, maintaining a, 15
nutmeg, 26

O
olives, 88
onions
    Chicken Zoodle Soup, 54
    Glazed Grain-Free Meatloaf + Crispy
        Onion Topping, 42
    Meat Pockets, 58
    Mimi's Little Veggie Trees, 122
    Rockin' Guacamole, 193
    Salsa, 186
Orange Berry Banshee, 133, *134*
Orange Dreamysicle Gummies, 96, *97*
orange juice
    Orange Berry Banshee, 133
    Orange Dreamysicle Gummies, 96
    Pineapple Phantom, 145
oranges, 25
oregano
    Easy Pizza Sauce, 178
    Mini Pizzas, 50

P
Paleo Piggies, 112, *113*
Pale-O's Cereal, *36, 37*
palm shortening, 18
pancakes, 34, *35*
papaya, 83, 232
Papaya"sick"les with Electrolytes, *82,* 83
paprika, 185, 190
parsley, 58
Parsnip Fries, *120,* 121
parsnips, 121
pasta
    Homemade Grain-Free Pasta, *162,* 163
    Mac 'N' "Cheese," 65
    Veggie Spaghetti + Meatballs, *44,* 45
pastries, 213
peaches, 145
"Peanot" Butter Chocolate Chip Cookies,
    208, 209

peas, 125
peppermint extract, 218
pepperoni, 62
Perfectly Pink Lemonade, 182, *183*
pimentos, 53
pineapple, 25, 145
pineapple juice
    Green Goblin, 138
    Strawberry Superpower, 141
Pineapple Phantom, *144,* 145
pizza
    Easy Pizza Sauce, 178
    Mini Pizzas, 50
    Pizza Crust, 160
    Pizza Pockets, 62
Pizza Crust, 160, *161*
Pizza Pockets, 62, *63*
plantains
    Cinnamon Maple Plantains, 33
    Critters on Logs + Homemade Sunflower
        Seed Butter, 111
popsicles, 83
positive reinforcement, 15
potato starch, 18
    Animal Crackers, 104
    Anything-But-Basic Vanilla Cupcakes +
        Bettercream Frosting, 214
    Cake Pops, 217
    Everyday Crackers, 151
    Give Peas a Chance Fritters, 125
    Grain-Free Corn Dog Dippers, 66
    Hot Dog Buns, 167
    Legit Sandwich Bread, 148
    Soft Pretzels, 107
    Sweet Potato Bacon Tots, 118
    Sweet Potato Slider Buns, 156
    Zucchini Sticks, 130
pretzels, 107
probiotic powder, 80
Pudding Dirt in a Cup, *204,* 205
pumpkin puree, 152
pumpkin seeds, 22, 152

Q
quesadillas, 61

R
radishes, 69
raisins, 111
Ranch, *172,* 173
raspberries, 25, 115
rice, 126
Rockin' Guacamole, *192,* 193
romaine lettuce, 133

S
Salsa, 186, *187*
sandwiches
    Grilled Cheese, 53
    Ham + "Cheese" Quesadillas, 61
    Liver Lovin' Turkey Burger Sliders, 57
sausage, 29
Sausage Quiche, *28,* 29
side dishes, 117–31
    BFF Brussels, *128,* 129
    Give Peas a Chance Fritters, *124,* 125
    Mimi's Little Veggie Trees, 122, *123*
    Parsnip Fries, *120,* 121
    Sweet Potato Bacon Tots, 118, *119*
    Veggie Rice + Gravy, 126, *127*
    Zucchini Sticks, 130, *131*
Silver Dollar Chocolate Chip Pancakes, 34, *35*
smoothies, 133–45
    Crantastic Trio, *136, 137*
    The Great Caped Grape, 142, *143*
    Green Goblin, 138, *139*
    Orange Berry Banshee, 133, *134*
    Pineapple Phantom, *144,* 145
    Strawberry Superpower, *140,* 141
S'mores, 206, *207*
snacks, 87–115
    Animal Crackers, 104, *105*
    Apple Cars + Caramel Dip, *114,* 115
    Critters on Logs + Homemade Sunflower
        Seed Butter, *110,* 111
    Graham Crackers, 98
    Great Grape Gummies, *90,* 91
    Gummy Worms, *102,* 103
    Ladybug Veggie Bites, 88, *89*
    Lala Truffles, 92, *93*
    Monkey Toes (Filled Dates), 108, *109*
    Orange Dreamysicle Gummies, 96, *97*
    Paleo Piggies, 112, *113*
    Soft Pretzels, *106,* 107
    Vanilla Wafers, *94,* 95
Soft Pretzels, *106, 107*
soup
    Bone Broth, 72
    Chicken Zoodle Soup, 54
spinach
    Crantastic Trio, 137
    Green Eggs + Ham Roll Ups, 38, *39*
    Green Goblin, 138
    Mint Chocolate Chip Ice Cream, 218
squash, 232. *See also zucchini*
    Chicken Zoodle Soup, 54
    Veggie Rice + Gravy, 126
    Veggie Spaghetti + Meatballs, 45
Standard American Diet, 12

strawberries, 25
    Strawberry Shortcake Bites, 221
    Strawberry Superpower, 141
Strawberry Shortcake Bites, *220, 221*
Strawberry Superpower, *140,* 141
Sunflower Seed Butter, 111
    Brownies, 202
    Mini Muffins, 152
    Monkey Toes (Filled Dates), 108
    "Peanot" Butter Chocolate Chip Cookies,
      209
    Sunflower Seed Milk, 181
Sunflower Seed Milk, 159, 181
sunflower seeds, 22
    Critters on Logs + Homemade Sunflower
      Seed Butter, 111
    Lala Truffles, 92
    Sunflower Seed Milk, 181
Sweet Potato Bacon Tots, 118, *119*
sweet potatoes, 232
    Crispy Sweet Potato Fish Sticks, 46
    Sweet Potato Bacon Tots, 118
sweet potato flour, 22
    Grain-Free Corn Dog Dippers, 66
    Sweet Potato Slider Buns, 156
Sweet Potato Slider Buns, 156, *157*
sweet potato starch
    Everyday Crackers, 151
    Legit Sandwich Bread, 148
    Sweet Potato Slider Buns, 156

T
taco shells, Crispy Taco Shells, 164, *165*
tapioca
    Dairy-Free Coconut Yogurt, 80
    Pizza Crust, 160
tapioca flour, 222
tapioca starch, 18
    Animal Crackers, 104
    Anything-But-Basic Vanilla Cupcakes +
      Bettercream Frosting, 214
    Banana Pudding, 75
    Cake Pops, 217
    Everyday Crackers, 151
    Graham Crackers, 99
    Grain-Free Corn Dog Dippers, 66
    Mini Muffins, 152
    Silver Dollar Chocolate Chip Pancakes, 34
    S'mores, 206
    Strawberry Shortcake Bites, 221
    Sweet Potato Slider Buns, 156
    Zucchini Sticks, 130
Teriyaki Meatballs + Daikon Noodles, *68,* 69

tomatoes
    Easy Pizza Sauce, 178
    Ketchup, 174
    Ladybug Veggie Bites, 88
    Mini Pizzas, 50
    Rockin' Guacamole, 193
    Salsa, 186
tomato sauce
    Cheesy Dip, 185
    Mac 'N' "Cheese," 65
    Salsa, 186
Tortilla Chips, *158*, 159
Tortillas
    Ham + "Cheese" Quesadillas, 61
    Pizza Pockets, 62
    Weeknight Paleo Tortillas, 155
transitioning, tips for, 12–13
treats, 201–23. *See also gummies*
    Anything-But-Basic Vanilla Cupcakes +
      Bettercream Frosting, 214, *215*
    Banana Pudding, *74,* 75
    Brownies, 202, *203*
    Brown Sugar Cinnamon Toasted Pastry,
      212, 213
    Cake Pops, *216,* 217
    Double Chocolate Layer Cake, 210, *211*
    Funnel Cakes, 222, *223*
    Mint Chocolate Chip Ice Cream, 218, *219*
    "Peanot" Butter Chocolate Chip Cookies,
      208, 209
    Pudding Dirt in a Cup, *204,* 205
    S'mores, 206, *207*
    Strawberry Shortcake Bites, *220,* 221
    Vanilla Wafers, 95
turkey
    Liver Lovin' Turkey Burger Sliders, 57
    Teriyaki Meatballs + Daikon Noodles, 69
turmeric
    "Cheese" Quackers, 100
    Cheesy Dip, 185

V
vanilla extract
    Anything-But-Basic Vanilla Cupcakes +
      Bettercream Frosting, 214
    Brownies, 202
    Dairy-Free Coconut Yogurt, 80
    Double Chocolate Layer Cake, 210
    Pudding Dirt in a Cup, 205
    Vanilla Wafers, 95
Vanilla Wafers, *94,* 95
vegetables, 122. *See also specific vegetables*
    Mimi's Little Veggie Trees, 122

Veggie Rice + Gravy, 126
Veggie Spaghetti + Meatballs, *44,* 45
Veggie Rice + Gravy, 126, *127*
Veggie Spaghetti + Meatballs, *44,* 45

W
waffles, 18
Weeknight Paleo Tortillas, *154,* 155
whipped cream, 197

Y
yellow squash
    Chicken Zoodle Soup, 54
    Veggie Rice + Gravy, 126
    Veggie Spaghetti + Meatballs, 45
yogurt, Dairy-Free Coconut Yogurt, 80

Z
zucchini, 232
    Chicken Zoodle Soup, 54
    Meat Pockets, 58
    Veggie Rice + Gravy, 126
    Veggie Spaghetti + Meatballs, 45
    Zucchini Sticks, 130
Zucchini Sticks, 130, *131*